The Crusades

A Captivating Guide to the Military Expeditions During the Middle Ages That Departed from Europe with the Goal to Free Jerusalem and Aid Christianity in the Holy Land

Free Bonus from Captivating History (Available for a Limited time)

Hi History Lovers!

Now you have a chance to join our exclusive history list so you can get your first history ebook for free as well as discounts and a potential to get more history books for free! Simply visit the link below to join.

Captivatinghistory.com/ebook

Also, make sure to follow us on Facebook, Twitter and Youtube by searching for Captivating History.

Contents

Introduction

It could be said that European kings and nobles in the Middle Ages were Crusade mad. The enormous amount of fighting men who periodically sailed off to the Near East to do battle with Muslims are evidence of the widespread popularity of overseas adventurism at the time. The notion of a Crusade, in which large armies assembled from various regions of Europe for the purpose of doing battle with Turkish and Arab Muslims, became so fixed that it was expanded to include Crusades against heretical European Christian sects.

There are many reasons why so many European nobles answered the call to take the cross, and they all are to be found in the complex organization of medieval feudal society, which evolved at varying rates among the diverse cultures of Europe.

When, in the Early Middle Ages, the centralized secular order in Western Europe crumbled with the collapse of the Roman Empire, there arose a plethora of quasi-states. These states were established among groups of people who shared common ethnic origins in the tribes of barbarians who had swept across the continent in waves. The absence of firm national or cultural borders meant that the states were constantly jockeying for dominance over lands—the major source of wealth. A culture of warfare arose, and it became ingrained in the organization of all of the disparate cultural groups.

The chaos of multi-ethnic and multi-lingual states in constant struggle with powerful and weak neighbors was balanced by a single unifying force, the Catholic Church. At times, the authority of the Church, led by the pope and organized under a hierarchy of ecclesiastical officials, came under fire. Disputes arose over the power of the Church to appoint secular officials and leaders. Also, in constant contention was the direct authority of the papacy over states producing revenues that the secular lords coveted.

In cases where diplomacy failed, and it did so more often than not, the leaders of states sallied forth from their fortified homes or castles to do battle with their neighbors, whether they be other secular lords or ecclesiastical officials, such as archbishops, bishops, or the pope himself, all of whom had armies at their disposal. As wealth was determined by territorial power, warfare was virtually constant. It was the determining factor in the organization of society.

Fighting became infused with the notions of honor, loyalty, and courage. Overlaying this were the Christian concepts of a just war, mercy, and morality. Thus, fighting men of the upper class and their retainers, prior to advancing into battle, engaged in Christian ritual prayer, pleading in advance for the forgiveness of any sins they might commit on the battlefield.

Because warfare was conducted for the purpose of acquiring land and expanding manpower for armies, a complex system of land ownership evolved. As it is said, to the victor go the spoils. In the Middle Ages, this did not generally mean the complete destruction of the estates of the defeated nobles. Rather, the defeated leader kept his rent-producing peasant farmers and turned over a portion of this income. The defeated leader and his fighting men were required to swear allegiance through the ritual of paying homage to the victor. The fealty of the defeated meant that the victorious lord could demand military service from an expanded army of knights and lower-class foot soldiers. The might of a lord was directly dependent on the quality and quantity of his own fighting men as well as those who, by means of conquest, served as his vassals.

Warfare was not the only way medieval nobles expanded their power. Through an intricate system of intermarriage among the powerful families, some semblance of order was obtained in which equally strong kings and nobles could, from time to time, let down their guard against avaricious neighbors, freeing them to attack lesser lords. Intermarriage was also important in securing alliances with non-vassal states should the need arise. Finally, intermarriage among the upper classes could support claims of authority by a noble or a king over the lands inherited by their offspring.

The Church was an integral part of this mix of interconnected alliances and vassal states. The papacy, at times, was equivalent to the noble landowners. Its lands or states were formed out of the same arrangement of vassal states from which armies could be raised. Owing an obligation to the pope, a kind of religious homage, were the archbishops, bishops, and abbots of monastic establishments. These officials were landowners in their own right and thus could call on their vassals to field fighting men when the need arose.

With a culture of warfare being prominent among the nobility of medieval Europe, it is easy to understand the attraction of engaging in wars in far-flung lands. When the pope called for the powerful leaders of Christendom to take up arms against the Muslims in the East, known as taking the cross of Christ, he was speaking to receptive ears. Not only were the nobles inclined to see their participation in the Crusades as an honorable way to demonstrate religious fervor, but they also saw them as a means of exercising their skill in fighting and, for the vassals, their loyalty to their overlord. The attraction of participating in the Crusades, perhaps the greatest one among certain kings and nobles, was the potential of acquiring lands, treasure, and fighters in a region that was untapped by the European feudal system.

The primary function of a knight was to fight. Even during intermissions between serious warfare, knights honed their skills and won honor in ritual tournaments. In one sense, the Crusades filled a vacuum for knights, much as the tournaments did. This explains why when a king or a noble was engaged in warfare at home in Europe, he felt no need to answer the pope's call to serve abroad. Ignoring the demands of the Church, even to the point of excommunication, was a reasonable way for a secular leader to exhibit his independence.

In retrospect, it is difficult to imagine why, over and over again, the call to fight in the Crusades resulted in the successful raising of huge forces of fighting men. The promises of adventure and wealth were strong motivators, that is for certain. The almost complete ignorance of the dangers of traveling so far to engage in war against a mysterious foe also explains in part the eagerness of Europeans to leave home and journey by land and sea to the Holy Land. It is certain that the Crusaders were oblivious to the fact that if they went overland to Jerusalem, they would have to face strong opposition on their way. They would have to depend on the locals along the way for supplies of food for the men and their horses and that they would have to overcome disease while making their way through virtually impassable terrain. If the Crusaders journeyed to the Holy Land by sea, they would inevitably be subject to shipwreck and attacks by hostile powers and pirates.

If the kings and knights who took the cross were unaware of what lay before them on their expeditions to the Near East, the vast majority of the Crusaders were even more lacking in knowledge. These were the foot soldiers, servants, and peasant workers who accompanied the wealthy knights. Among the foot soldiers were trained crossbowmen and spear-bearing infantry. They were drafted from amongst the lower classes of the nobles' and their vassals' estates. Similarly, the enormous number of servants, required for all kinds of duties from feeding the horses, tending to the armor and swords, setting up camp, and managing horses and carts carrying supplies, were undoubtedly unaware of the trials and tribulations they would encounter abroad. The death toll among the lower-class Crusaders, particularly the noncombatants, was not recorded, as the chroniclers of the time would have seen their significance to the Crusades as being very minimal.

There were two Crusades that fell outside the usual expeditions of wealthy, aggressive, adventure-seeking knights. The People's Crusade of 1096 and the Children's Crusade of 1212 were organized among the lower classes who were convinced by charismatic leaders to set off to the Holy Land and deal with the Muslims either through force or through conversion to Christianity. The lower-class Crusaders were entirely unequipped to do either, let alone succeed in making the long journey east with limited resources.

Whether they were motivated by the promise of adventure or wealth, many Crusaders when they reached the Holy Land settled into a life that mirrored that which they led at home. On their journeys to the East, in the absence of Muslim opponents, they attacked Jews, Byzantine Christians, and non-supportive kings and nobles. While on marches to the East and when they had settled in the Holy Land, the Crusaders, in lulls between engaging with real or imagined enemies, squabbled and fought amongst themselves. Because they lived to fight, many of the Crusaders behaved abominably toward their fellow Christians. The knights of one noble were likely to turn on those of another in disputes over the division of spoils or their superior's tactics in war. These were men who thrived on fighting, so when the enemy was not in sight, they drew swords with each other over even the most minuscule of differences. The impossibility of controlling the Crusaders is evident in several of the expeditions.

Because the Crusaders were primarily fighters, their equipment and tactics are of great importance to understanding their successes and failures in dealing with their opponents. The arms and armor used by medieval knights during the Crusades evolved throughout that period of time to become increasingly elaborate. In the First Crusade, mounted warriors wore a suit of chainmail from head to foot and carried shields or bucklers and simple broadswords. As time passed, plates of hardened or carburized iron were added to protect vulnerable parts of the body. The most well-known armor, the full plate suit, was not common until well after the end of the Crusades.

The arming sword, or knightly sword, was a single-handed, double-edged, cruciform sword that was utilized for thrusting or cutting in combat. In the late 12th century, the arming sword came in two forms. As armor became increasingly dominated by of the use of plates, a blunt, short, heavy version of the arming sword was used to inflict blunt trauma through armor, and a narrow-pointed version was used to pierce the enemy's armor. Eventually, both types were replaced by the broadsword or longsword that was wielded by one or both hands. A third type of sword, a single-edged sword, similar to a Persian scimitar, might have been the preferred weapon of some knights. These swords were weighted toward the hand so that the blade could be wielded with lightning speed. Knights also carried daggers, which were essentially short double-edged swords that could be carried at the small of the back or girdle.

Foot soldiers carried maces or clubs with a wooden or metal shaft and a head of stone, iron, or steel. Maces with longer shafts were also used by cavalrymen. Because maces were easy to make, they became the favored weapon of the peasant class.

Along with maces and axes, the foot soldiers wielded a spear or a lance that had a wooden shaft with a sharpened head at the end, either made from the wood itself or as a forged metal attachment. By the time of the Crusades, spears were held by soldiers rather than hurled at the enemy. Depending on the country of origin, the Crusaders had specialized weapons. For example, the Danish carried broadaxes, and pikes, which were 3- to 6-meter-long (around 10 to 19.5 feet) thrusting weapons, were used by the infantry of Flanders and Scotland.

During the Crusades, in pitched battles or planned military encounters on a prearranged battleground, the commander would deploy infantrymen to stand against the opposing infantry. Any break in the lines was exploited by a charge of the knights. If they were successful in this charge, the knights would turn their horses and attack the enemy infantry from the rear or attack the enemy's mounted soldiers head-on. In the first stage of a pitched battle, the goal was to incapacitate individuals among the enemy forces and thus compel a retreat. It was in a retreat that Muslim and Crusader armies faced the greatest danger. Foot soldiers and cavalries were particularly vulnerable if they were attacked from behind, and it was thus in a retreat that many were killed outright. In the time of the Crusades, wounding a soldier was an effective way for their elimination from further combat because, for the most part, most of the wounded died.

The Arabs and Turks who fought against the Crusaders employed foot soldiers with spears as their first line as did the Crusaders themselves. Behind them would be mounted warriors dressed in chainmail and carrying swords, shields, and lances. Muslim cavalry depended on swiftness, and their mounted warriors were less encumbered by heavy armor and swords. The Saracen mounted archers were particularly effective against the Crusader forces. The Crusader crossbowmen were likewise effective on the battlefield and in shooting down upon enemies from siege towers or castle walls.

The Welsh and English were especially skilled in the use of the single-piece longbow (some bows later developed a composite design), and they managed to shoot arrows that could penetrate chainmail. French and German longbowmen were somewhat less talented with the awkward weapon. It took years of practice to perfectly handle the longbow, which in the hands of the most adept could shoot about six arrows per minute. This rate of fire was far greater than competing weapons like the crossbow. The advantage of the crossbow was that it had greater penetrating power and did not require the extended years of training.

The history of the Crusades is complicated. Events in Europe impacted the makeup of the Crusader armies, and events in the East affected the makeup of the Muslim forces. For the Christians, leadership and the depth of allegiance of the nobles to one to another were primarily responsible for battles being won or lost. Honor and greed played equal parts in their successes and failures. Behind the entire enterprise, which endured over three centuries, was the Church, which was no different from secular powers in switching allegiances in the interest of exerting authority and increasing the value of its treasury.

Due to the rise of the Christian Church in the era of the decline of the Roman Empire, the faithful had been encouraged to make pilgrimages to the Holy Land to gaze upon the sites which marked the life of Christ and his mother Mary, as well as his disciples and the early Christian saints. By the 12th century, the route recommended to the pilgrims had become established enough for a German ecclesiastic to write *Guide to the Holy Land* (1172). He described for his limited audience of literate Christians what they could expect to see in Jerusalem, such as the column of the scourging of Christ and the grotto in which the cross was found. He wrote about the Christian sites in Bethlehem, Nazareth, and Damascus. The volume of faithful pilgrims who flocked from Europe and cities in the Byzantine Empire was certainly substantial. It was the safety of these pilgrims and the protection of these venerated sites that was the professed motivation for dispatching the armies of the European kings and nobles to fight in the East. However, there were other motives at play. Among these were regional conflicts over territorial expansion, ecclesiastical differences with secular authority, doctrinal conflicts within the Church, and greed and human aggression.

Chapter 1 – The First Crusade (1095-1099) –The Pope Calls the Faithful to Arms

In the last two decades of the 11th century, the Byzantine Empire's capital, Constantinople, was on the verge of collapse. Invasions from abroad and internal warfare threatened the existence of the empire. Emperor Alexios I Komnenos, who was crowned on April 5th, 1081, was immediately challenged by an incursion into the empire by a force of Norman freebooters from Italy under the leadership of Robert Guiscard. Guiscard, who had set out from Normandy around 1047 with a small following of mounted soldiers, had settled in the Byzantine province of Calabria in Italy by means of force. Through incredible military prowess, he gained authority over the entire population of Normans who had settled before him in southern Italy. After conquering most of Byzantine Sicily, Guiscard sailed with his troops across the Adriatic Sea. In 1081, he defeated the Byzantine soldiers in the outpost at Dyrrhachium, located in present-day Albania. The Normans then chased the defeated Byzantine forces into Greece, where they were threatened with complete annihilation.

It was only by seeking assistance from abroad that Alexios was able to save his provinces in the southern Balkans. He relieved the pressure Guiscard was exerting on the Byzantine soldiers by paying Holy Roman Emperor Henry IV 360,000 gold pieces to step up his attacks on the Normans in Italy. The Italo-Normans were allied with Pope Gregory VII, who had made an enemy of the Holy Roman emperor. Henry IV had claimed that it was his right to appoint church officials—archbishops, bishops, and abbots —or invest ecclesiastical offices within his empire. In effect, this meant that he could demand his share of revenues from ecclesiastical estates. Pope Gregory claimed that the right to fill ecclesiastical offices was his alone. In 1076, Henry was excommunicated for his intransigence in what is known as the Investiture Controversy.

Henry decided to invade Italy to settle his differences with the pope. He attacked the pope's Italo-Norman allies in southern Italy and assumed authority over states directly under the authority of the papacy. In Rome, a party of Italians and Germans arose to combat the pope's broad claim of power. In 1080, a synod of monarchist churchmen unseated Gregory and replaced him with Pope Clement III. Two years later, Emperor Henry attacked Rome. After a siege of seven months, the city fell. Pope Gregory, who refused to accept his replacement as pope, fled to Monte Cassino and then later to Salerno along with his court. Clement III was installed on the papal throne in 1084. A year later, Gregory died in exile.

The Normans, who were the pope's allies in Italy, faced a formidable enemy in Emperor Henry IV, who was prepared to take over their estates. Robert Guiscard was thus forced to abandon his expedition against the Byzantines in the Balkans and return to Italy. This ended the crisis faced by the Byzantine emperor.

The followers of Gregory VII regarded Clement as a usurper, or an antipope. After Gregory's death, they elected a line of popes opposed to the Holy Roman emperor. Among them were Pope Victor III and Urban II, the latter who served from March 1088 to his death in July 1099.

Urban, who was French by birth, spent the early years of his papacy outside Rome. He was kept away by Antipope Clement III, who was under the protection of the Holy Roman emperor. Among Urban's early successes were the arrangement of diplomatic marriages between powerful Italian families and securing the support of England against his rival pope in Rome.

The ascendancy of Urban's papacy began at the Council of Piacenza, a synod of ecclesiastics and laymen, which was held in the first week of March in 1095. This was a large meeting, consisting of 200 bishops, 4,000 other church leaders, and some 30,000 laymen. As well as denouncing the Antipope Clement III, the council considered the request put forth by an embassy from Byzantine Emperor Alexios I Komnenos. He sought help in recovering Byzantine territory that had been lost by the expanding eastern empire of the Seljuk Turks.

The Sunni Muslim Seljuk Turks had risen to power in Persia and spread like lightning across vast swaths of Asia Minor in the 11th century. After adding Armenia and Georgia to their empire, the Seljuks, under their leader Muhammad bin Dawud Chaghri, more commonly known as Alp Arslan, engaged with the Byzantine forces. The invasion came to a head with Alp Arslan's rout of the Byzantines in the Battle of Manzikert in August 1071 in eastern Asia Minor. The Byzantine emperor at the time, Romanos IV Diogenes, was captured. The defeat threw the Byzantine court into disarray. When he was freed, Romanos' opponents deposed, blinded, and exiled him. He died a slow death from an infection brought on by the removal of his eyes. He was succeeded first by Michael VII Doukas, who was forced to abdicate in 1078 by his generals, and then Nikephoros III, who was also forced to abdicate.

With the coronation of Alexios I Komnenos in 1081, a measure of internal order was restored to the Byzantine Empire, but the presence of the Turks in what had once been Byzantine territory was a constant irritant to the Byzantine emperor and his nobility and presented an unending threat to the stability of the empire. Thus, the call for help went out to Pope Urban II.

Although no action was taken on Alexios' request for military aid at the Council of Piacenza, it was critical to the unfolding of events at the subsequent council of ecclesiastics and laymen held in Clermont, France, that same year. At Clermont, Urban II met with a large congregation of French and Italian bishops to deal with reforms within the Church. In the midst of this council, on November 27th, 1095, Urban II preached to a large crowd of peasants, nobility, and clergy assembled in a field outside Clermont. His persuasive arguments for dealing with the enemy of the Byzantines was framed around the responsibility of Christians to rid the Holy Land of infidels.

Five versions of Urban's sermon were written down later. These were influenced by subsequent events, so none of them can be considered to be the exact words of the pope himself. In one version, he is claimed to have said that his flock of Christians should cease fighting among themselves, cease hating one another, and "Enter upon the road to the Holy Sepulchre; wrest that land from the wicked race."

It is reported that his call for liberating the Holy Land from heathens was greeted with chants from his audience. "It is the will of God! It is the will of God!" No doubt Urban expected this enthusiastic outburst because prior to giving his speech, he had traveled widely in southern France to have preliminary talks with ecclesiastical and secular lords about his idea for a Crusade.

One account of Pope Urban's speech says that he promised, "All who die by the way, whether by land or by sea, or in battle against the pagans, shall have immediate remission of sins." This was to be so because the "despised and base race" who worship demons should never conquer "a people which has the faith of omnipotent God...made glorious with the name of Christ."

Pope Urban set out several reasons for calling for a Crusade against the Turks. He said that it was the duty of Christians to protect their brothers in faith in the East. However, there was also an expansionist tinge to his speech. He believed that the reason there was so much infighting in the West was due to the growing peasant population depending on diminishing quantities of productive land. Not only were the peasants suffering, but their landlords were also being stretched thin because their rental income in the form of agricultural produce was diminishing. Urban also understood the situation that the non-inheriting, impoverished sons of nobles were in. He praised their military prowess and offered them a way to distinguish themselves on the battlefield by engaging in the Crusade. He urged them to stop engaging in raids on their neighbors, in which they sought to demonstrate their knightly skills. Rather, the pope urged them to take up arms with their fellow Christians against the infidels in the East. The opportunity to win remission from their sins was an added bonus. The pope promised those who took the cross that upon their death, a smooth and hasty elevation from limbo or purgatory would occur, allowing them to live an eternal life in heaven.

A successful Crusade against the Muslims in the Holy Land would make it possible for all pilgrims to travel to the holiest of Christian sites without being harassed by non-believers. Christian pilgrims to Jerusalem, said Urban, had suffered awful torture and murder at the hands of the Seljuks. Female pilgrims had even been raped. Urban's condemnation of the Muslims was based on secondhand reports and was in all likelihood to have been somewhat of an exaggeration. Urban reported that the most abominable act suffered by Christians at the hands of the Turks was having their navels perforated and their intestines drawn out and then attached to a stake. The hapless victims were forced to walk around until all of their intestines were pulled out and they died. It is unlikely that Urban was citing firsthand accounts of this way of slowly killing Christians. In all probability, he had most likely been told the story by one of his advisors who, in turn, had adapted it from the story of the martyrdom of St. Erasmus in 303 CE. The Christian Erasmus had suffered extreme torture at the hands of the pagan Romans. The details of this were repeated and magnified in texts recounting the final moments in the lives of Christian martyrs. St. Erasmus, said his biographers, was first enclosed in a barrel into which spikes had been inserted. The barrel was then rolled down a hill. Erasmus' injuries were miraculously healed by an angel. The Romans then coated Erasmus with tar and set him alight, but thanks to the intervention of the angel, he survived. At a loss as to how to dispatch the apparently immortal Erasmus, the Romans slit open his belly, pulled out his intestines, and wound them up on a barrel until he finally died. There was great similarity between the story of the worst torture the Christians supposedly endured at the hands of the Turks and the original tale of Erasmus' martyrdom at the hands of the Romans.

From the earliest days of Christianity, pilgrimages to the Holy Land had been encouraged by Church authorities. Since the fall of the Holy Land to the Muslims in the 7th century, though, pilgrims were exposed to difficult conditions. Nevertheless, the faithful flocked to the East in such numbers that a guidebook was written for them around 1172 by an unknown German named Theoderich. The book outlined an itinerary which took in all the Christian holy sites, such as the Grotto of the Annunciation at Nazareth, the Church of the Holy Sepulchre in Jerusalem, and the town of Jaffa where pilgrims could recall the resurrection of Tabitha by the Apostle Peter.

Historians have delved into the possible motives Urban may have had in making his momentous call for a Crusade against the Muslims in the Holy Land. Clearly, the idea had been planted in his head with Alexios' plea for help in ridding his empire of Turks. Some historians suggest that Urban was motivated by a desire to reunify the Eastern and Western Churches under his sole leadership. In 1054, theological differences and disputes over authority had led to what became known as the Great Schism. The splitting of what is today the Roman Catholic Church and the Eastern Orthodox Church was in the West understood as a direct affront to the authority God bestowed on the pope; of course, the East also felt that it was an affront to the authority of their patriarch.

Some historians have interpreted Urban's call for a Christian Crusade as an attempt to dispose of his rival, Antipope Clement III, who was the spiritual leader of a powerful contingent of imperialist nobles loyal to Henry IV. It may have been Urban's hope that before enthusiastic Crusaders set off for the East, they would swarm down into Italy and deal with Clement III, who was installed in Rome, and his major supporter Henry IV. In sum, if all of Christendom's major warriors were to take up the Crusade many of Urban's problems with the secular world would vanish, at least for a while.

The chroniclers who in the following years wrote down versions of Urban's speech were all in agreement that his sermon was incredibly effective. They all likely exaggerated the reaction among the audience, though. This is probably true for the account that when the pope ended his speech, hundreds in the audience sewed cloth badges with the cross on them onto their tunics, thus indicating that they were immediately taking the cross and joining the Crusade.

The well-trained fighters who accepted Urban II's call to fight against the Turks were convinced to take up arms in the name of God by the many itinerant preachers who fanned out over the countryside taking the message to members of regional noble families and other aristocrats. The actions of three hermit monks living in the forest near Laval, southwest of Paris, are typical of the call to arms during the Crusades. Robert of Arbrissel, Vitalis of Mortain (also known as Vitalis of Savigny), and Bernard of Thiron, like many of their clerical colleagues upon the urging of the pope, quit their lives of seclusion and set out on the road to sway the hearts and minds of all who heard their fiery sermons. Urban himself spent nine months spreading the word in large and small towns in France. By means of letters to bishops and abbots, he spread the word to England, Flanders, and the Italian cities of Genoa and Bologna. In some of his letters, he was specific about the goal of the Crusade. It was to expel the infidels from Jerusalem and turn the city into a Christian community.

One of the first men to take up Urban's cause was Peter the Hermit. The story of this priest of Amiens, France, was recorded in a history called the *Alexiad*. It was written in the late 1140s or early 1150s by Alexios I Komnenos' daughter, Anna Komnene. She wrote that Peter had once attempted to make a pilgrimage to the Holy Land, but he was turned away by the Turks, who he claimed had mistreated him. He became a charismatic, revivalist preacher to peasants, paupers, and perhaps a few knights. There is no historical document confirming that Peter the Hermit was present when Urban delivered his sermon at Clermont in 1095, but thereafter, Peter the Hermit added the call for a Crusade to his addresses to his followers. He used his own experience at the hands of the Turks to inflame thousands to take up the cross and follow him to the Holy Land.

Peter's following of peasants grew rapidly. Suffering from years of drought and disease brought on by poor harvests, peasants and paupers who were wards of the Church were drawn to the Crusade as a means of escaping a life lived in poverty or neglect. A number of minor knights were also enlisted to support what became known as the People's Crusade or the Pauper's Crusade.

Contingents of Peter's army of indigents and impoverished knights marched east toward the Rhine. Spurred on by inflammatory rhetoric by emulators of Peter, a group under Rhineland Count Emicho of Leiningen demonstrated their furor against non-Christians in the spring of 1096, by leveling Jewish communities in France and Germany and massacring their inhabitants. When they arrived at Worms, Emicho's army demanded that the resident Jews convert to Catholicism or either be expelled or killed. About 800 members of the Jewish faith were murdered. Emicho and his followers claimed to be exacting revenge against a race and a religion responsible for the death of Christ. This justified their theft of the money of the Jewish population to finance their Crusade. In Mainz in May 1096, Emicho's army killed over a thousand Jewish people. Smaller towns in the region suffered similar attacks. Having completed his rampage against the Jewish population in the Rhineland, Emicho and his troops set out for the East.

When Emicho's adventurers reached Hungary, their supply of money to purchase food was depleted. So, they turned to pillage. The Hungarians fought back with skill and determination, killing most of Emicho's followers. Emicho himself fled to his home in Germany, where he was roundly criticized for failing to fulfill his vow to capture Jerusalem.

Peter's Crusaders finally assembled on April 12th, 1096 at Cologne, where he intended to continue preaching and gather more supporters. Impatient to get to the Holy Land, some undisciplined French peasant Crusaders rushed off to Hungary, then Belgrade, and then finally to Niš in the Byzantine Empire. They were eventually followed by Peter's 40,000 Crusaders, whom he led from Cologne to Hungary. A dispute over spoils arose at the town of Zemun, and the Crusaders rioted and killed 4,000 of its inhabitants. When they arrived at Niš, another dispute arose, and the Crusaders were routed, and a quarter of their number was killed. The remaining members of Peter's army pushed farther into the Byzantine Empire and were eventually escorted to Constantinople. The emperor Alexios I Komnenos, unable to feed an army of virtually penniless outsiders, quickly arranged for them to be taken across the Bosporus Straits. They were deposited in Asia Minor on August 6th, 1096, with a friendly warning from the emperor to stay away from the fierce Turks in Anatolia.

The peasant Crusaders proceeded to pillage and destroy the weakest Seljuk towns. When they reached Nicomedia, about 100 kilometers (around 62 miles) east of Constantinople, a dispute between the German and Italian Crusaders and French Crusders broke out, and both sides elected new leaders who took their followers on raids against different Turkish strongholds. The People's Crusade had now ceased being under the sole control of Peter the Hermit. He returned to Constantinople in the hopes of securing aid from the

Byzantine emperor. While he was away, the remaining Crusader army, which numbered around 20,000, departed on October 21, 1096, to attack Nicaea. Along the way, they were ambushed by the Turks and were forced back to their camp to join the women, children, and incapacitated who had been left behind. The Turks succeeded in slaughtering most of the Crusaders; only about 3,000 were able to find refuge and be eventually rescued by the Byzantine army. Peter himself waited out the winter of 1096/1097 in Constantinople. When Pope Urban's Crusaders under the leadership of princes, nobles, and knights reached the city, he joined them on the journey east.

While the People's Crusade was precipitously moving east, Pope Urban's army of princes was departing in Europe. The pope, prior to his speech at Clermont, had secured the support of two of the most powerful leaders of southern France, Adhemar of Le Puy and Raymond IV, Count of Toulouse. The French king, Philip I, was ineligible to join the cause as he had been excommunicated by Pope Urban at the Council of Clermont in 1095 for the sin of bigamy. However, he encouraged his brother, Hugh, Count of Vermandois, to enlist a skilled group of knights from lands east of Paris. They were joined by some of the survivors of Emicho's aborted Crusade. Hugh's army departed from the port of Bari in southern Italy in August 1096, the date set by Urban for the journey east. In Bari, Hugh met the Norman Prince of Taranto, Bohemond I, who was also preparing to head east with a contingent of soldiers.

Impatient to enter the fray against the Turks, Hugh didn't wait for his fellow Crusader. A boastful man and one who turned out to be a failure as a commander, Hugh wrote to the Byzantine emperor announcing his imminent arrival in Constantinople. His letter was recorded by Anna Komnene, "Know, Emperor, that I am the King of Kings, the greatest of all beneath the heavens. It is my will that you should meet me on my arrival and receive me with the pomp and ceremony due to my noble birth." Despite Hugh's bravado, his arrival in the Byzantine Empire was pathetic. Most of his ships sank in a storm off Dyrrhachium, and many of his knights drowned. He managed to swim ashore where he was arrested by the Byzantine commander of the outpost. Brought to Constantinople, Hugh was forced to swear his fealty to Alexios Komnenos.

The Duke of Lower Lorraine, Godfrey of Bouillon, was inspired by Cluniac monks and took the cross. To finance his expedition, he had to sell two of his estates and borrow money against the value of his castle. In his large army of knights, archers, and foot soldiers were his two brothers, Eustace and Baldwin, both without estates to their name. Perhaps in anticipation of settling in the Holy Land and gaining great riches there, Godfrey took along his wife and children. He set out in August on the land route to Constantinople. When he reached Hungary, his army was waylaid by King Coloman, who, after his encounter with the People's Crusade, was wary of foreigners attacking his people. In negotiations with King Coloman, Godfrey agreed to turn over Baldwin, Baldwin's wife, and children as hostages to provide security that a repeat of the chaos did not occur. Godfrey's army behaved admirably and refrained from fighting the Hungarians. The hostages were released, and the Crusaders were allowed to proceed. When they reached the Sea of Marmara, Godfrey lost control of his army, and they pillaged the area for some days. After restoring order, he led his troops to Constantinople. They arrived there on December 23, 1096. Emperor Alexios demanded Godfrey's homage, which he secured after threatening to attack the Crusader's camp outside the city walls. Alexios hurriedly had Godfrey and his retinue ferried across the Bosporus in order to avoid any possibility that the Crusaders might attack Constantinople rather than head off to the east.

The next army of Crusaders arrived in Constantinople on April 9, 1097. These men were even more unwelcome by Emperor Alexios. They were led by the Norman Bohemond, the son of Robert Guiscard, the archenemy of Byzantium. Bohemond himself had stayed in Greece after his father departed, and he had defeated Alexios' army in two battles. It was only through enlisting the aid of the Seljuk Turks that Alexios was finally able to push the Normans under Bohemond into a retreat in 1083.

However, Bohemond was there at Alexios' door again, having raised a large contingent of Crusaders that sailed from Bari to the coast of Bulgaria and then traveled by land to Constantinople. Once there, Bohemond judiciously swore an oath of fealty to Alexios, who then provided ships to carry Bohemond's troops across the Bosporus where they joined Godfrey's troops.

Among the first of the French nobles to take up Urban's challenge to free the Holy Land was Raymond IV of Toulouse. An extremely devout man, it was his hope to die in Jerusalem. This may have been due to his age as he was 55, which was close to the end of an average lifespan in the Middle Ages. He may also have desired forgiveness for his sins of twice marrying women to whom he was closely related. For these infractions of Church law on consanguinity, he had been excommunicated.

Raymond set out with his army of Crusaders at the end of October 1096. He was accompanied by his wife and child, as well as Adhemar, bishop of Le Puy. Raymond marched overland to Dyrrhachium. From there, his army moved into Byzantine territory. When they faced shortages of food, they pillaged the farms and towns along their route to Constantinople. In the absence of Raymond, who had gone ahead to negotiate with Alexios, the French Crusaders were defeated by a large contingent of Byzantine soldiers who were charged with maintaining order among the unruly Crusaders. Meanwhile, Raymond cleverly avoided swearing allegiance to Alexios, preferring instead to pledge his support on the condition that Alexios himself would lead the Crusade. When Raymond's army arrived in Constantinople, they were hastily ferried across the Bosporus to avoid any repeat eruptions of violence on Byzantine soil.

Another leader of an army of Crusaders was Robert II, Duke of Normandy, who was the eldest son of William the Conqueror.

Although he had illustrious roots, Robert was in dire straits financially when he answered Urban's call. He mortgaged his land to his brother, King William II of England, to pay for his expedition. Among his retinue were knights from England and Scotland as well as Normandy. Included in their number were his cousin, Robert II, Count of Flanders; his brother-in-law, Stephen, Count of Blois; and a priest, Fulcher of Chartres. The latter was to write a chronicle of the First Crusade in which he included a version of Pope Urban's sermon at Clermont.

Robert led his army south from Normandy, crossing the Alps and traveling to Calabria in southern Italy. Not wanting to risk a winter voyage across the Adriatic Sea, Robert camped there for the winter. When the weather improved in the spring of 1097, a tragic accident occurred. The first vessel to leave the port of Brindisi broke in two. Some 400 fighting men drowned. This disaster motivated some of Robert's men to desert. The remaining troops eventually arrived in Dyrrhachium and moved east to Constantinople, arriving there in early May. Robert did as his fellow Crusaders had done. He swore allegiance to Alexios, and his army was taken across the Bosporus.

Chapter 2 – The Armies of the First Crusade Engage with the Enemy

Modern historians have come up with approximate numbers for the Crusaders who set out from Europe for the Holy Land in the First Crusade. They calculate from the available evidence that there were as many as 130,000 participants. Of these, about 13,000 were knights and 50,000 were trained foot soldiers, which included crossbowmen and spear-bearers. The remaining 67,000 people were the non-fighting peasants, servants, and assorted noncombatant family members of noble households, which included women, children, clergymen, and, of course, a good number of enterprising male and female camp followers. To field a knight in battle required a good number of support staff—armorers; dressers; men to feed, curry, and saddle horses; and cartmen to transport a knight's tent, food, cooking utensils, luggage, and food for several horses. The knight, and his family if they came along, required cooks and servants. The more important knights and members of royal households also brought along the clerks required for carrying out the duties of a small traveling bureaucracy and priests to deliver the sacrament of Holy Communion before the knights went into battle.

In the mass of Crusaders were several clerics to advise the knights on political and religious matters. The priests, clerics, and clerks in turn required a number of servants to assist them in their duties and provide them with adequate accommodations and food.

The loss of numbers due to starvation, disease, desertion, and battles with local peoples on the way through Europe left only about 50,000 Crusaders to assemble in 1097 in the vicinity of Nicaea in Asia Minor.

Emperor Alexios, who many expected to lead the Crusade, opted to stay in his palace in Constantinople. He did send a few of his troops to accompany the Crusaders through Anatolia to help them recover Byzantine states that had been captured by the Turks. Some of the European adventurers, believing that the recovered land was up for grabs, laid claim to it instead. Squabbles arose when they were denied ownership. This episode and the failure of Alexios to provide any kind of leadership and his refusal to provide meaningful military help to the Crusaders turned the knights against the Byzantines. They came to regard them as perfidious, avaricious schemers lacking in a deep commitment to the Christian faith.

The Crusaders surrounded the city of Nicaea in May of 1097. They took advantage of the absence of the Seljuk leader, Kilij Arslan I. He had taken a temporary leave of Nicaea, believing that the assembled Crusaders were as harmless as the peasants of the People's Crusade who his troops had recently slaughtered. Upon his return, Arslan led his army out of the city to engage with Raymond IV, Count of Toulouse's army of Crusaders. Arslan, however, was forced to retreat behind the city walls after learning that Raymond's knights were extremely capable and ferocious fighters. They lopped off the heads of Arslan's soldiers and drew up catapults to knock down the walls of Nicaea. The siege was resisted until Emperor Alexios, having made a secret deal with the Turks, arrived with his army, marched into the city, and laid claim to it for his empire. This confirmed the Crusaders' belief that the Byzantines were not to be trusted.

Like all major military expeditions, the Crusaders, because of their vast numbers, faced logistical problems with respect to the supply of food for the knights, foot soldiers, and the enormous train of noncombatants. Foodstuffs and fodder for horses were purchased or pillaged as the army made its way east. The sparsely populated lands of central Anatolia, through which the main body of the Crusaders passed, was not rich in agricultural produce. Most of the farmland in the region was cultivated by subsistence farmers who provided their landlords with meager rents in the form of grains and hay gleaned from their dry, rocky fields, as well as wool and meat from their livestock. The lack of food and fodder forced the main body of the Crusader army to hasten through Anatolia. Their numbers dwindled as this forced march exhausted many, making them susceptible to disease and death by starvation.

Two of the lesser leaders with Crusader armies, Baldwin of Boulogne, the brother of Godfrey of Bouillon, and Tancred, a Norman from southern Italy who had joined his uncle Bohemond's army, were dispatched to the fertile plains of Cilicia in the southeastern corner of Anatolia to discover if there were sufficient food and fodder to support the main body of Crusaders. Baldwin and Tancred each led small contingents of knights numbering between 100 and 300 men. In spite of having only a few fighting men at his disposal, Tancred succeeded in taking from the Turks the town of Tarsus. When Baldwin arrived, he persuaded Tancred to push on farther east while he organized the occupation of Tarsus. An army of about 300 Italo-Normans arrived at the gates of Tarsus. These soldiers were a straggling contingent of Tancred's army. Baldwin refused them entry into Tarsus, and the Turks took advantage of Baldwin's diminished forces and murdered as many of the Crusaders as they could capture. Some of Baldwin's own knights objected to their leader's rejection of a fellow Crusader army. To vent their frustration and anger, they turned on the remaining Turks in Tarsus and massacred them.

When Baldwin left Tarsus and caught up with Tancred, their two bands of knights squared off against each other, as Tancred's men were indignant at Baldwin's treatment of their countrymen. A few knights were killed in the confrontation, and many were injured. Crusaders fighting among themselves was simply a continuation of the European knightly code of conduct in which the preservation of honor coupled with high-strung, often brutish behavior, was the root cause of squabbles and physical violence. As can be seen, many of the Crusader knights were motivated more by the promise of an adventure than a deeper need to serve the interests of their Christian religion. Baldwin and Tancred negotiated peace and went off in different directions. Baldwin, who had formed an alliance with the Christian Armenian minority in the eastern coastal region of Anatolia, was seen by them as a convenient liberator from the Seljuk Turks.

Antioch, the first goal of the Crusaders when they arrived in the Near East, was incredibly well defended by the Turks. It had extensive, formidable walls interrupted by some 400 towers from which archers could shoot down on a besieging army. On October 20, 1097, the Crusaders laid siege to the fortified city. The Crusaders' optimism for a quick victory faded as winter set in with little progress being made in the fighting with the Turks. Supplies ran short, leading to deaths from disease and starvation; many deserted as well. The siege showed signs of failure when the Crusaders were unable to intercept supplies that the Turks brought into the city. Turkish reinforcements arrived. Their two attempts in December 1097 and February 1098 and their own siege of the Crusaders in June 1098 failed to lift the Crusaders' siege. On all three occasions, the Turks were attacked by the Crusaders on the outskirts of Antioch. In a show of superior military skills, the Crusaders decimated the Turkish relief armies.

It was with the assistance of Firouz, a wealthy Armenian Christian convert to Islam, that the Crusaders finally gained access to the city of Antioch in May 1098. Firouz helped the small detachment of

Crusaders to scale the tower he controlled before they opened a gate for the main army of Crusaders to pour through. As they stormed into the city, the Christian inhabitants of Antioch simultaneously rose up against their Turkish overlords. What happened next was a massive slaughter of the Turks, allowing the city to come under Christian control. The Crusaders and the Christians of Antioch were fearful that huge numbers of Turkish troops would soon arrive on their doorstep. The premonition of doom was alleviated somewhat when a local priest related that he had had a dream in which Christ had come to him. He was assured by the Son of God that all would be well in five days. The morale of the Crusader knights was also raised when Peter Bartholomew, a pilgrim from Provence, told them that he had been visited by the spirit of Saint Andrew. The good saint had pointed out to Peter Bartholomew the spot in the Church of Saint Peter where the lance that had pierced the side of Christ at the Crucifixion was buried. Some eager knights entered the Church of Saint Peter and dug up the lance. The holy trophy was held high by a cleric, who, along with a subsequent chronicler of the First Crusade, Raymond of Aguilers, led the Christian army out of the city to engage the relief column of the Turks. It was believed that the assistance of this sacred talisman was responsible for the success of the Crusaders in completely destroying the Turkish force.

With the city of Antioch firmly under Christian control, the Prince of Taranto, Bohemond I, unilaterally claimed the city for himself. He was opposed in this by Raymond IV, Count of Toulouse, who reminded him that both had taken an oath of fealty to the Byzantine emperor. This meant that Antioch was rightfully the property of Emperor Alexios. Bohemond denied that he owed anything to the Byzantine emperor because the emperor had sent none of his troops to assist in the taking of Antioch. Raymond eventually conceded that Bohemond's assumption of the title of Prince of Antioch was legal and just. Doubtless, Raymond anticipated his own assumption of ownership over a more important Crusader goal, Jerusalem.

While Antioch was under siege, Baldwin and his small contingent of knights in Anatolia organized an expedition to assist the Armenian Christian ruler of Edessa, Thoros, in dealing with the Seljuk Turks who were marauding towns near the city. Two Armenian leaders, Fer and Nicusus, joined with Baldwin in February 1098 as he set out to the east to take Edessa. After engaging with the Turks in the countryside around Edessa and occupying the city, Baldwin took advantage of a religious dispute among the Christians of Edessa. Thoros was overthrown and murdered in a riot precipitated by nobles who objected to his Greek Orthodox Christian faith. The theological dispute involved differences in opinion on the true nature of Christ. The insurgent nobles were Monophysites, or believers that Christ has a single divine nature. The Greek Orthodox Church, on the other hand, holds that Christ was both divine and human. With a vacuum of leadership in Edessa, the Christian population accepted Baldwin as the ruler of their city and the surrounding region. Baldwin proceeded to consolidate his hold on what was to become the first Crusader state. He used force, diplomacy, and subterfuge whenever the need arose. He cemented his alliance with the Armenians by marrying the daughter of an Armenian noble.

Raymond of Toulouse, who had ceded Antioch to Bohemond, left the city with his army and laid siege to the city of Ma'arrat al-Numan, located in modern-day Syria, on the road south to Damascus in late 1098. Shortly before, Ma'arrat had been subject to attack by a small contingent of Crusaders, and the Crusaders had been beaten off by an inferior number of Turkish soldiers. So, when Raymond's force arrived, the Turks of Ma'arrat were confident of their victory. Because the Crusader army arrived at Ma'arrat in late November, a protracted siege was out of the question. With the onset of winter, food supplies were expected to diminish, forcing the retreat of the Crusaders back to Antioch.

The Turkish militia in Ma'arrat held their city for two weeks during which the Crusaders built a siege tower. Shooting down the tower archers succeeded in clearing a section of the wall, and Raymond's infantry was able to gain a foothold on the wall on December 11. To avoid a battle which the Crusaders were clearly going to win, the citizens of Ma'arrat negotiated a surrender in which it was agreed that they would be allowed safe conduct out of the city. The Christian soldiers, breaking the agreement and the ideals of their faith, massacred the Muslims. It was even reported that the starving Christian fighters engaged in cannibalism. The chronicler Fulcher of Chartres wrote;

> I shudder to tell that many of our people, harassed by the madness of excessive hunger, cut pieces from the buttocks of the Saracens [Muslims] already dead there, which they cooked, but when it was not yet roasted enough by the fire, they devoured it with savage mouth.

While the Turks were engaged in defending Antioch, Ma'arrat, and other towns in Syria against Christian attacks, the control of Jerusalem had changed hands. In what is now modern-day Palestine, two groups of Muslims had been contending for ascendancy. The Fatimid Caliphate, centered in Egypt, held sway over much of the region prior to the arrival of the Seljuk Turks from Persia. Under the direction of the vizier for the Fatimids, al-Afdal Shahanshah, the Fatimids forced the Seljuks out of Tyre in 1097, and in 1098, they took Jerusalem. A year later, on June 13, 1099, the Crusaders launched their attack on the Egyptian Muslim forces occupying Jerusalem. They succeeded in breaching the outer walls but were stymied by a lack of ladders in their assault on the inner walls. The lack of supplies for a full-scale siege was remedied when a flotilla of supply ships from Genoa arrived in the port of Jaffa. The resupplied Crusaders constructed the necessary ladders and built siege towers and catapults. Upon receiving intelligence that al-Afdal had left Cairo with a large force and was on his way to relieve the siege of Jerusalem, the Crusaders hastened their attack. Their eventual success was predicted by a priest who had a vision. He was told that God wanted his forces to fast for three days and then walk barefoot around Jerusalem. With this optimistic message taken to heart, the

Crusaders pushed their catapults to the walls of Jerusalem from which they rained down arrows on the defenders. Ladders were brought up, and the Christian army flooded into the city on July 15. Soon, the streets were clogged with the rotting bodies of dead Muslims. On July 22, Godfrey of Bouillon assumed the honorific of Defender of the Holy Sepulchre, and Arnulf of Chocques, one of the clerics in his entourage, was appointed as the Latin Patriarch of Jerusalem.

To ensure that Jerusalem would remain under Christian control, Godfrey of Bouillon led 10,200 troops out of the city on August 10. With bare feet, the Crusaders marched south, accompanied by Arnulf of Chocques carrying a relic of the True Cross, the cross upon which Jesus was crucified, which had been recently discovered by Arnulf of Chocques. In Jerusalem, the former leader of the People's Crusade, Peter the Hermit, led the Christians in prayer.

Outside the city of Ashkelon, also known as Ascalon, on the Mediterranean coast of modern-day Israel, the combined Crusader armies of Godfrey of Bouillon, Raymond IV of Toulouse, and Robert II of Normandy launched a surprise attack on al-Afdal's 20,000 troops while they were sleeping. More than half of al-Afdal's army perished. Al-Afdal managed to escape the massacre by boarding a ship and sailing back to Egypt.

The fall of Jerusalem allowed Godfrey of Bouillon to create the Kingdom of Jerusalem of which he became the ruler. At first, the kingdom was a loose federation of towns and cities that had been captured during the Crusade, but at the height of its power in the 12th century, the kingdom included the territory of modern-day Israel, Palestine, and the southern parts of Lebanon. Three other Crusader states were founded around this time, located farther north—the County of Tripoli under Raymond IV of Toulouse, the Principality of Antioch under Bohemond, and the County of Edessa under Baldwin of Boulogne. Godfrey's system for organizing the Kingdom of Jerusalem followed the pattern of feudalism in Europe. He created fiefdoms for his most important followers who were then obliged to supply knights and foot soldiers for the defense of the kingdom. Unlike in Europe, the fiefdoms were not self-sustaining agricultural communities. In the place of revenue from in-kind rents, the fiefdoms in this region were financed directly from the treasury of Jerusalem. From Jerusalem, Godfrey launched attacks in 1100 on Acre, Ascalon, Jaffa, and Caesarea, forcing these cities to become tributaries.

On July 18, 1100, Godfrey died unexpectedly. The circumstances of his death are not clear. According to a contemporary Arab chronicler, Ibn al-Qalanisi, it is said that he was killed by an arrow in a battle at Acre. Two contemporary Christian writers say that he became sick in Caesarea and died. Of course, there were rumors that he was poisoned, but this was standard fare at the time in the accounts of the death of the powerful, who invariably had real and imagined enemies.

Chapter 3 – The Aftermath of the First Crusade

With Edessa firmly under his control, Baldwin of Boulogne and some of his knights set out on a pilgrimage to the Christian city of Jerusalem. Along the way, they suffered casualties in battles with the Muslims. The small band of knights reached their destination on December 21, 1099. After visiting the holy places, Baldwin returned to Edessa. When Godfrey, ruler of the Kingdom of Jerusalem, died in 1100, there was a struggle among his retainers for the throne. The Latin Patriarch of Jerusalem, Arnulf of Chocques, sent a delegation to Edessa, asking that Godfrey's brother, Baldwin, return posthaste to Jerusalem and take on the role as the leader there. He accepted the invitation and set out on October 2, 1100, with about 200 knights and perhaps double that number of foot soldiers. He was welcomed in Jerusalem where he took on the title of prince and was subsequently crowned king on Christmas Day, 1100. He put Edessa under the control of his cousin, Baldwin of Le Bourg.

After the conquest of Jerusalem, many of the Crusaders returned home. The garrison under King Baldwin is estimated to have consisted of as few as 300 knights. Fulcher of Chartres wrote, "We scarcely dared to assemble our knights when we wished to plan some feat against our enemies." Nevertheless, under Baldwin's leadership, the area around Jerusalem was pacified. The arrival of about 5,000 Norwegian Crusaders under King Sigurd I Magnusson in 1100 served to alleviate the crisis caused by the shortage of fighters. The Crusaders solidified their position by capturing the ports of Acre in 1104 and Beirut in 1100 and Sidon in 1111. This permitted the Kingdom of Jerusalem to be supported by maritime trade with Genoa, Pisa, and Venice. The greatest contributions to the treasury, however, were revenues derived from pilgrims, taxes on Arab caravans moving through the kingdom, and subsidies from Europe.

Baldwin was intent on expanding the territory of the Kingdom of Jerusalem. Among the many expeditions against the Turks and the Egyptian Fatimid Muslims was one against Damascus. However, in the Battle of Al-Sannabra, Baldwin was routed by the Seljuk Turks. As was usual at the time, Baldwin solicited the help of his enemy's enemies. He thus formed an alliance with the dissident Turks. In 1115, he joined with a Turkish leader, Toghtekin, to fight off the Seljuks making incursions on the northern borders.

Freed from threats to the north, Baldwin led an expedition in the fall of 1115 across the Jordan River to deal with the Egyptians. He engaged in a program of castle building, constructing them in territories as they fell under his control. From these castles or military outposts, which stretched from the Gulf of Aqaba nearly to the Dead Sea, Baldwin monitored the movement of the Egyptians and secured a steady source of income from caravans engaged in trade between Egypt and the Far East along the Silk Road.

On an expedition into Egyptian territory, where he captured towns in the Nile Delta, Baldwin fell ill. He was transported back to the frontier where he died on April 2, 1118. His successor as King of Jerusalem, chosen by the knights holding fiefdoms in the kingdom, was Baldwin de Bourg, Count of Edessa. King Baldwin II ruled Jerusalem for thirteen years. During much of his reign, he was absent from Jerusalem, tending to the military needs of the

Principality of Antioch. Its army was virtually annihilated by the Muslims on June 29, 1119. Baldwin had some successes in dealing with the crises in the north. In 1131, he fell ill at Antioch. He was taken back to Jerusalem where he died on August 21.

During Baldwin II's reign, a process of assimilation occurred in the Holy Land. Fulcher of Chartres reported that the small number of European residents in the Holy Land soon acquired skills speaking Greek and Arabic and looked upon themselves as being more Levantine than European. It seems that the Christian minority were tolerant of the Islamic majority; they, in turn, were quite happy to husband their flocks unmolested by raiders as well as to render taxes to the Christians, which was at a rate less than other Muslims had to pay in territories controlled by the Fatimids and the Turks. The Christians avoided tensions with the Muslims in their kingdom by letting them worship unmolested and making no effort to convert them.

Because the Crusaders were spread thinly throughout the kingdom, the routes traveled by pilgrims were often dangerous. A major massacre of Christians occurred at Easter in 1119. A band of Muslims from Tyre struck at a large band of pilgrims, killing around 300 and taking the others as slaves. This and other acts of violence against pilgrims deeply upset the French knight Hugues de Payns, Count of Champagne. He obtained the blessings of King Baldwin II and the Latin Patriarch of Jerusalem to establish a military monastic order dedicated to the protection of pilgrims. The order took its name from the Temple Mount. On it stood the captured Al-Aqsa Mosque. Entombed in the earth beneath the mosque were, it was believed, the ruins of King Solomon's Temple. Hugues de Payns' new monastic order, which at first consisted of nine knights, adopted the name Poor Fellow-Soldiers of Christ and of the Temple of Solomon. They are more popularly known as the Knights Templar or more simply the Templars.

Before Jerusalem fell to the Crusaders, a Benedictine monk, Gerard Thom, known as Blessed Gerard, had received permission from the

Arabs to found a hospice for pilgrims visiting the holy sites. The need for caring of the pilgrims grew, and Gerard built the Hospital of St. John in the 1060s. Even when Jerusalem was under siege by the Crusaders and the Christians were expelled, Gerard and his few followers were permitted to remain in the city to tend to the sick. When the Crusaders under Godfrey occupied Jerusalem, Gerard's good works were recognized. Later, King Baldwin I and his successor Baldwin II granted the charitable group substantial sums of money. As Gerard received more assistance, he was able to expand his operation to include subsidiary hospitals along the pilgrimage routes in Europe as well as in the Near East. Further, as well as tending to sick and indigent pilgrims in the Holy Land and Europe, Gerard and his fellow monks began to provide military escorts for pilgrims from their arrival in the ports of modern-day Palestine, Israel, Syria, and Lebanon to the holy city. This work demanded that Gerard's men adopt a disciplined military function similar to that of the Templars. They received official recognition and independence from all secular authority through a papal bull issued by Pope Paschal II in February of 1113. Known as the Order of St. John, the Knights Hospitallers followed a monastic rule adapted from that of St. Benedict and St. Augustine. With money flowing in from Europe, the Knights Hospitallers acquired castles and established garrisons manned by knights along the major pilgrimage arteries.

The successes of the First Crusade were to stand as the highpoint in Christian expeditions to the Holy Land. The setbacks that followed the establishment of the Kingdom of Jerusalem were to lead to a series of Crusades that were marked by a combination of Christian nobles' infighting and failures of leadership while simultaneously the Muslims began to unify under stronger leadership which resulted in the loss of Christian control over the Levant.

Chapter 4 – The Second Crusade (1147-1149) The Beginnings of the Kingdom of Jerusalem

Amity between the Muslims and the Christians may have existed in Jerusalem and other major cities in the area, but in the countryside, the kingdom was fraught with constant turmoil. Muslim fighters raided from within and without the kingdom.

In the fall of 1144, Joscelin II, Count of Edessa, formed an alliance with the Ortoquid Turks, also spelled as Artquid Turks, a dissident clan whose land was sandwiched between the Sultanate of Rûm in Anatolia and the Mosul Turks in modern-day Iraq. The Ortoquid soldiers and the Christian knights marched out of Edessa to engage with Imad ad-Din Zengi, the Turkic leader of both Mosul and Aleppo. Zengi outmaneuvered the troops from Edessa, defeating them and began to besiege the city once it no longer had an army to defend it. On Christmas Eve, Zengi's men breached the weak defenses of Edessa. His army proceeded to slaughter the inhabitants until Zengi ordered his men to stop the massacres. Later, the Latin prisoners were executed, but the native Christians were unharmed.

The struggle to keep the Turks and the Fatimids at bay in the Crusader kingdoms began to collapse with the fall of Edessa in 1144. When news of the disaster at Edessa reached Europe, Pope Eugene III called for the Second Crusade. Eugene was the first pope to come from the Cistercian monastic order. The Cistercians were a particularly austere order of monks who followed the monastic rule of St. Benedict in 516 CE. Eugene was elected pontiff on the same day as his predecessor Pope Lucius II succumbed to a wound sustained by a stone thrown at him by an unruly mob egged on by the insurgent Commune of Rome, a government modeled on the old Roman Republic.

The most influential cleric at the time, the Cistercian Bernard of Clairvaux, although objecting to the choice of Eugene, inserted himself into papal affairs to such an extent that he virtually ruled the Church.

Embroiled in a conflict over the extent of papal authority over secular affairs, Eugene was forced to vacate the city of Rome to escape the wrath of the noble class, retreating northward to France. It was there that he proclaimed, in a papal bull in December 1145, his call for the Second Crusade. His decree, *Quantum praedecessores*, was directed at King Louis VII of France. The French king immediately began preparations for an expedition to the Holy Land. In Germany, the self-styled King of the Romans, Conrad III (he was never crowned as Holy Roman emperor, however), and his nephew, Frederick Barbarossa, were likewise persuaded to join the cause after hearing Bernard of Clairvaux preach about the Crusade. Things got off to a rocky start when the assembly of German Crusaders fell victim to the mania of killing by massacring the Jews in Mainz and Würzburg. The leader of the Cistercian Order, Bernard of Clairvaux, hastened to Germany and demanded that the undisciplined Crusaders cease their attacks on the Jewish community.

Bernard succeeded in terminating the chaos among Conrad's German Crusaders. Upon his urging, they set out from home and traveled, more or less peacefully, overland to Constantinople. They arrived there on September 10, 1147. The violence that accompanied the arrival of the first Crusaders from Europe was repeated again. The Byzantine army defeated Conrad's forces in a battle outside the walls of Constantinople. Byzantine Emperor Manuel I Komnenos quickly arranged for the Crusaders to be transported across the Bosporus. If Conrad and his army were expecting to receive assistance from the Byzantine emperor, they were sorely disappointed. Manuel had already headed off war with the Turks occupying Anatolia by negotiating a truce with them. This meant that he and his army could not march east in support of the Crusaders.

While Conrad was preparing for his Crusade, the pope expanded his call for the removal of Muslims from Christian lands, declaring that the Reconquista of the Iberian Peninsula, which was still under control of the Moors, was a legitimate Crusader objective. English knights who had taken the cross in response to Pope Eugene's bull while sailing south to enter the Mediterranean Sea were diverted to the city of Porto in Portugal. There, they were persuaded to ally themselves with King Alfonso I of Portugal in a siege against the Moorish city of Lisbon. The English Crusaders were promised the spoils of conquest and thus had a particularly strong motive for taking part in the Reconquista. The protracted siege of Lisbon lasted from July 1, 1147, until the Islamic Moors surrendered in October of that year. With their newfound wealth from pillaging, some of the English Crusaders settled in Portugal, becoming permanent landholders; some even joined in the liberation of other Portuguese cities with the objective of sating their passion for fighting and obtaining the spoils of victory. The diversion of the Reconquista left only a few of the English Crusaders eager to board ships and sail to the Holy Land.

Not waiting for the arrival of the French Crusaders, Conrad's expeditionary force pushed on into Seljuk Turk territory in Anatolia. His army did not fare as well as those previously commanded by Godfrey of Bouillon, Baldwin of Boulogne, and Raymond IV of

Toulouse in the Battle of Dorylaeum in the First Crusade. Much of Conrad's army perished in the second Battle of Dorylaeum on October 25, 1147. The disastrous reduction in the size of Conrad's following of knights continued even after his army was joined by the French Crusaders. They arrived too late to be of much assistance in dealing with the Turks.

The French Crusaders, under the command of Louis VII, had departed from Metz on June 15, 1147. They traveled overland following the route used by Conrad some months earlier. The assembled French Crusader army was ferried across the Bosporus without gaining any support from Emperor Manuel. However, as mentioned above, the combined armies of Conrad and Louis VII were no match for the powerful Turks. After the second Battle of Dorylaeum, Conrad himself retreated to Constantinople while some of his troops in the company of the French sailed to Antioch. After a short stay in the Byzantine capital, where Conrad was singularly unsuccessful in obtaining the aid of Emperor Manuel, the King of the Romans sailed off to join his army in Syria.

The French Crusaders under the leadership of Louis VII reached Antioch with many troops lost in skirmishes with the Turks and even more succumbing to starvation. The combined Crusader forces did not head east to dislodge the Turks from Edessa, which was the intended focus of Pope Eugene's Crusade to begin with. They instead moved south to Damascus, a target preferred by the King of Jerusalem, Baldwin III, and the Knights Templar.

With Baldwin's army backed up by Louis' troops in the vanguard and the remainder of Conrad's army in the rear, the Crusaders attacked Damascus from the west. Their approach to the city was strongly opposed by the Turkish army who took advantage of the Crusaders' mistake of choosing a heavily forested route to approach. The Crusaders did succeed, although at great cost, in pushing forward, and on July 24, 1148, they drove the Turks back into the city. They renewed their attack, this time from the east. However, bickering broke out among the Christian knights whose varied allegiances made a unified attack impossible. The siege of Damascus was called off primarily because the Crusader lords who had taken up fiefdoms around Damascus refused to cooperate. With the Turks momentarily expecting reinforcements from as far away as Mosul, proceeding with the siege seemed a fruitless task to several knights. The disputes over strategy among factions of the Crusaders led to Baldwin III and his troops marching off in a huff back to Jerusalem. King Louis and Conrad reluctantly followed. Neither had succeeded in winning anything approaching honor in their Crusade, nor had they even attempted to liberate Edessa as the pope had expected. In Jerusalem, the Crusaders continued their squabbling. Conrad departed for Constantinople to again pursue a private alliance with Emperor Manuel, and King Louis VII, determining that there was no profit to be had in remaining in the Holy Land, returned to France with his army in 1149. Conrad also took himself and his troops back to Germany.

The aftermath of the fiasco of the Second Crusade consisted of consolidation of Christian control over the Levant orders—the Templars and the Hospitallers—the Christians constructed some fifty castles and fortifications. These military establishments were necessary as part of the continuing war of attrition, in which neither the Muslims nor the Christians had gained the upper hand in the territories surrounding the major cities.

King Baldwin III of Jerusalem was struggling with his mother, Queen Melisende, who had served as co-ruler with her son—both were crowned in 1143. He first assumed sole power in 1152 but relented in the face of opposition to his unilateral action. He agreed to put the dispute over control of the kingdom before a court. The court ruled that Baldwin would keep his authority over Galilee, and Melisende would rule the richer Judea and Samaria, which included Jerusalem. Baldwin, not content with the decision, attacked the supporters of Melisende in the south and forced Melisende to seek refuge in the Tower of David in Jerusalem. The two eventually reconciled with Melisende taking on the role of principal advisor to

Baldwin and regent when he was away from Jerusalem on his frequent campaigns.

Baldwin was faced with Fatimid Muslims to the south and Seljuk Turks in the north. Both were enemies that had not been dealt with decisively by the Second Crusade. In the north, Aleppo and Edessa were firmly in the hands of Nur ad-Din, the son of Imad ad-Din Zengi, who had died in 1146. Nur ad-Din's successes in fighting off the Crusaders, particularly in the Siege of Damascus, inspired him to attack Antioch, which was under the control of its prince, Raymond of Poitiers. Raymond was defeated in battle and killed, leaving Nur ad-Din in control of most of the territory of the Principality of Antioch. With Nur firmly established in the north, Baldwin III, in 1153, launched a campaign against the Fatimid city of Ashkelon, a Mediterranean port to the west of Jerusalem. Baldwin's army besieged Ashkelon from both the land and the sea. His army prevailed after a lengthy siege, and the city came under Christian control. It was assumed into the County of Jaffa, in which some of the wealthiest Crusader seigneuries, or feudal lordships, were held.

Upon Baldwin's death in February 1163, Amalric I, the second son of Melisende, became King of Jerusalem. His first campaign against the Fatimids in Egypt was launched in 1163. It was partially successful against an enemy that was, at the time, embroiled in dynastic squabbles. Amalric extracted large sums of tribute before calling off his knights and foot soldiers from their looting. In 1164, Amalric again moved against Egypt, and like his earlier expedition, the goal was not to liberate Christian holy sites from the control of the Muslims but rather to enrich his own treasury and the wealth of his knights. No substantial territorial gains were secured, however. In his absence from Jerusalem, Nur ad-Din defeated a large Christian army in the Battle of Harim (August 12, 1164). Amalric rushed north to the aid of the Christians and managed to save Antioch from the Turks.

In his final incursion into Egypt in 1168, Amalric, having to deal simultaneously with the complication of interference by the

Byzantines, made a truce with the new sultan of Egypt, Salah ad-Din. Salah ad-Din, or as he was known to the Christians Saladin, was a Sunni Muslim born in Tikrit in modern-day Iraq. He had risen through the ranks in Nur ad-Din's army. He was dispatched to Egypt in 1164 to interfere in a Fatimid power struggle. Staying on there, he succeeded in winning advancement in the Isma'ili Shia Muslim army and government of Egypt. In 1169, in a rare instance of intersect accord, he was appointed vizier. He proceeded to undermine Fatimid authority, and after the death of the last Fatimid leader, he abolished the Caliphate and aligned Egypt with the Abbasid Caliphate centered in Baghdad. In the following years, Saladin's attempts to conquer the Crusaders failed, but he was successful in defeating the Turks in Syria, taking Damascus in 1174, Edessa and Aleppo in 1175, and in 1183, he assumed an expanded title, indicating that he was not only Sultan of Egypt but also of Syria. In effect, he succeeded in surrounding the Christian Kingdom of Jerusalem. He strengthened his position by making a treaty with the by now virtually powerless Byzantines to fight jointly against the Christians in the Holy Land.

In the pitched Battle of Hattin near Tiberius, located in modern-day Israel, on July 4, 1187, Saladin, leading some 20,000 to 40,000 troops, routed the Christians who fielded about 18,000 to 20,000 men led by 1,200 knights. Thousands of Christian soldiers were killed; only about 200 Crusader knights left the battlefield alive. All of the captured Templars and Hospitallers were beheaded. Guy of Lusignan, crowned King of Jerusalem in 1186, was captured and imprisoned. After this massacre, disheartened Crusaders fled from their castles to hide behind the protective walls of Jerusalem. The safety of this haven ended when it, too, fell to Saladin in early October of 1187. Although Saladin freed thousands of the Christians and allowed the purchasing of the freedom of thousands of other Christians, perhaps as many as 15,000 Christians were sold as slaves. Refugees from Saladin's attacks flocked to the only remaining cities under Christian control—Antioch, Tyre, and

Tripoli. Tyre became the object of Saladin's next campaign. It was saved by the Christians, thanks to the strategic skills of Conrad of Montferrat, who arrived from Europe just in the nick of time. He organized the defenders, cleverly destroyed Saladin's fleet blockading the port, and sallied forth from the city and routed Saladin's army.

Chapter 5 – The Third Crusade (1189-1192) – The King's Crusade

The fall of Jerusalem to Saladin caused outrage in Europe. The newly elected pope, Gregory VIII, believed that the loss of the Holy Land was God's punishment for the sins of Christians. He issued a bull calling for a Crusade to restore all of the pilgrimage sites under Christian control.

Henry II of England and Philip II of France, as well as a number of French and Flemish counts, agreed to begin preparations for the Third Crusade that became known in history as the "King's Crusade." The pope convinced Conrad III's successor and cohort during the Second Crusade, Frederick Barbarossa, who was actually crowned as the Holy Roman emperor in 1155, to join the campaign. He took up the cross at Mainz on March 27, 1188. The 67-year-old Frederick was in his own right the most powerful secular leader in Europe. His empire stretched from the Baltic to Italy and from Hungary to France. As such, he was able to enlist an enormous number of knights who owed him fealty. Modern historians estimate the size of his army as ranging from 100,000 men, including 20,000 knights, to a lesser number around 14,000 men and about 4,000 knights.

Frederick Barbarossa led his knights, infantry, and their servants overland, down through Hungary and Serbia to Greece and off into Thrace. There, he came up against the troops of Byzantine Emperor Isaac II Angelos. Isaac, acting in concordance with a treaty he had concluded with Saladin, fought the Crusaders to stop their progress to the east. Frederick's large army quickly defeated the Byzantines, and they were granted safe passage through Constantinople in the fall of 1189 and traveled on to Syria. However, Frederick was killed in an accidental drowning that occurred just short of his goal of Antioch. Many of his troops then deserted to make their way home to Germany. The already weakened German troops that chose to carry on succumbed to disease, thinning their forces even more. As a result, when the German army arrived at Acre, it consisted of as few as 5,000 soldiers. Frederick's successor as the leader of the German forces, his son Frederick VI of Swabia, buried his father in Syria and prepared to recommence attacks on the Muslims.

On July 6, 1189, Henry II, King of England, died before the launch of the new Crusade. He, along with Philip II, King of France, had taken the cross in 1188. Henry's son, Richard I, had independently taken the cross in 1187 in his office as Count of Poitou in France. Richard, also known as Richard Coeur de Lion and more commonly known as Richard the Lionheart, launched an unsuccessful insurgency against his father in 1173. Some historians suspect that his mother, Eleanor of Aquitaine, instigated this revolt. Prince Richard left England and entered his own lands in France, where he firmed up his control by making an alliance first with King Louis VII of France and then with his successor Philip II, known as Philip Augustus. The climax of Richard's revolt came when his army faced off against Henry II's knights in a battle in Ballans in the Nouvelle-Aquitaine region on July 4, 1189. Richard emerged as the victor. After the passing of his father two days later, he declared himself

King of England, and on September 3, 1189, he was crowned at Westminster Abbey.

With money in the royal treasury, some of which had been collected as a ten percent tithe levied by Henry II for preparation of the new Crusade after Saladin's victory at Hattin in the Holy Land, Richard was able to raise a substantial Crusader army, which included knights recruited from his English fiefs as well as his dependencies in France, which included Normandy, Aquitaine, Gascony, and Brittany. The departure of Richard's force was delayed because he had to set loyal supporters in place to protect his authority in England and manage his French possessions while he was away. Both Philip and Richard were aware of the danger of attacks on their territories during their absence on the Crusade—both being protective of their suzerainty over parts of France—so it was necessary for them to both depart their kingdoms to ensure that there was no imbalance should war break out.

Richard and Philip, allied only for the purposes of taking the cross, took their armies first to Sicily. The citizens of Messina, fearing the presence of a vast number of foreign troops, revolted. They were soon put down by Richard, who attacked Messina and looted and burned the city. Tensions between Philip, Richard, and the ruler of Sicily, King Tancred, reached a boiling point, but the three managed to sign a peace treaty resolving some of their issues. The major bone of contention was the imprisonment of Richard's sister, Joan of England. As was common in medieval diplomacy, she had been married to King William II of Sicily in 1177. When William died in November of 1189, his throne was usurped by his cousin, the current King Tancred. The treaty between Philip, Richard, and Tancred secured Joan's freedom, the restitution of her dowry, and established that Richard's nephew and heir, Arthur of Brittany, would marry one of Tancred's daughters.

Royal and noble betrothals and marriages were the cause of much friction throughout the Middle Ages, and a dispute broke out between Philip and Richard over the latter's engagement to Philip's sister, Alys. She was, according to rumors at the time, once the mistress of Richard's father. The French and English kings, perpetually suspicious of each other's motives, agreed to the termination of Alys' betrothal to Richard. In her place, Berengaria, the daughter of the King of Navarre, was promised to Richard. Her suitability as a wife for Richard was, of course, decided on the basis of diplomacy based on her familial connections. In 1190, she was brought to Richard in Sicily by Richard's mother, Eleanor of Aquitaine. There, Richard's sister Joan and Berengaria became fast friends. They both boarded a ship in Richard's fleet that set out from Sicily headed toward the Holy Land.

The ship carrying Joan and Richard's fiancée, Berengaria of Navarre, ran aground on Cyprus. Ashore, their safety was threatened by the island's governor, Isaac Komnenos, the great nephew of Byzantine Emperor Manuel I Komnenos. To come to the rescue of his kin, Richard turned his fleet toward Cyprus, invading the island and deposing Isaac. Having almost lost his betrothed, Richard hastened to sanctify their union, marrying Berengaria in Limassol, Cyprus, on May 12, 1191.

Before the English and French Crusaders reached the coast of the Holy Land, the King of Jerusalem, Guy of Lusignan, who had been released from captivity by Saladin in 1188, had begun a campaign against Saladin's army to restore parts of his kingdom that had been recently lost to the Muslims. He set his eyes on Acre, then one of Saladin's major garrisons. With the Crusader army virtually wiped out in the Battle of Hattin, Guy could only field a small army of about 8,000 infantry and some 600 knights. His initial surprise attack in 1189 failed. He set up camp outside Acre and awaited the arrival of the Crusader fleets. A contingent of Normans from Sicily pulled into the port of Acre, but they abandoned their mission when they learned of the death of their king, William II, on November 11, 1189. They were replaced by a flotilla of Crusaders from Northern Europe that blockaded the port. Guy's forces successfully repelled an attack by Saladin but not before suffering severe losses.

Saladin, with reinforcements brought in by sea and by land, continued to engage with Guy's army, which was strengthened with the addition of Crusaders who had arrived from Europe. In early 1191, Guy, attempting to take advantage of the partial destruction of the walls of Acre, launched an attack. Sadly, for him, it failed. In February, Saladin succeeded in a landward advance. Breaking through the Crusaders' lines, he was able to relieve the defenders of Acre.

In April of 1191, King Philip II's fleet of chartered Genoese ships arrived in the port of Acre, and his army joined in the siege of Saladin's garrison in the city. King Richard I's troops arrived aboard some 100 ships in June. Being the first to arrive in the Holy Land, King Philip took the lead. He built siege engines and trebuchets, or catapults, and trained them on the walls of Acre. Whenever a breach in the walls was made, Saladin's army attacked the Christian encampment. This distraction allowed the defenders of Acre to repair the walls. The standoff came to an end when the garrison offered to surrender to the Crusaders. A peace treaty was negotiated in which Saladin agreed to exchange prisoners with the Crusaders and make three substantial ransom payments of the imprisoned garrison. At the end of July, Philip set sail and returned to France. His departure from the Holy Land was necessary as a crisis loomed in the succession to the leadership of one of his most important dependencies in France, which he feared would be vulnerable to English attacks.

In August of 1191, Richard I, now the sole commander of the Third Crusade, marched south with as many as 4,000 knights and 14,000 infantrymen. Saladin's army followed him. His archers harassed the Crusaders from the rear, but Richard's soldiers held off, turning back to fight them head-on. The discipline of King Richard's men was even remarked upon by Muslim chroniclers of the Crusades. Following the command of their leader Richard, the Crusaders did not respond to being harried by Saladin's archers. The Muslim archers were, in any case, hampered by their use of the recurved bow. The arrows they shot from a distance either fell short of their mark or if they struck Richard's men, were, for the most part, ineffective in penetrating their armor. In contrast, the Crusader archers used the much more powerful and considerably more accurate crossbows. Their shorter bolts were much more deadly at a greater distance and were capable of penetrating the armor of Saladin's soldiers.

Moving south along the coast of modern-day Palestine, Richard's army camped adjacent to the forest of Arsuf. Saladin drew up his army on the open plain inland from the forested region, his forces numbering around 25,000 soldiers. Most of them were mounted archers and light cavalry with a minority being foot soldiers. Modern historians estimate Richard's army at somewhere in the region of 20,000. They were comprised of English, Norman, French, and other European Crusaders, along with fighting men drawn from the knights of the Kingdom of Jerusalem. The entire force was guarded in the rear by the Knights Hospitallers.

On September 7, 1191, Richard's army left their camp, with the Knights Templar standing in the vanguard. They were followed by contingents of troops organized by their European country of origin and, once again, was followed by the Knights Hospitallers. As they approached the forest of Arsuf, Saladin's warriors, concealed among the trees, poured out and attacked Richard's army. As was their custom, archers and spear throwers cleared a path for the thundering horde of mounted archers and sword fighters. As the anonymous author of the contemporary chronicle, *Itinerarium Regis Ricardi*, put it, "In truth, our people, so few in number, were hemmed in by the multitudes of the Saracens, that they had no means of escape."

The repeated attacks of Saladin's troops did not stop Richard's advance. The rearguard Hospitallers, however, did not hold firm to their orders. Impatient at being harried from behind, they turned around and advanced against Saladin's men. Richard, understanding that the Hospitallers were bound to be destroyed in this attack, turned his whole army around and launched an all-out battle. The

Crusaders, all of them impatient to get into the fray, completely routed Saladin's army. Richard halted his advance and after reorganizing his troops led a second charge. His personal ferocity in the battle was recorded in the chronicle *Itinerarium*. "The extraordinary king, cut down the Turks in every direction...wherever he turned, brandishing his sword, he carved a wide path for himself." He cut down the enemy "like a reaper with his sickle." After regrouping his men for a second time, Richard launched a third attack, after which Saladin's troops retreated.

The Battle of Arsuf proved the mettle of the Crusaders. Saladin was not invincible as his reputation would have it seem after all. In the aftermath, Richard's Crusaders took the port of Jaffa. Saladin withdrew his troops from several of his garrisons along the coast of modern-day Palestine, and the one he did retain, Darum, modern-day Deir al-Balah, in the Gaza Strip, was later taken by force by King Richard. With the coastal region secure, the Crusaders were poised to take Jerusalem.

In November 1191, Richard's Crusaders advanced on Saladin's forces in Jerusalem. He requested aid from Conrad of Montferrat, the ruler of Tyre. Conrad had been an off-again, on-again supporter of Richard. One of the reasons for this was his allegiance to Byzantine Emperor Isaac II Angelos. After assisting Isaac II in putting down a revolt, Conrad had arrived in the Holy Land in 1187. He entered Tyre at the moment when its ruler was on the verge of surrendering the city to Saladin, who, buoyed by his victory at Hattin, was on the march north. Conrad took control and fought off two sieges by Saladin. In the negotiations for the surrender of Tyre, Saladin offered to release Conrad's father, William V of Montferrat, and pay off Conrad. Conrad was not tempted. Problems arose for Conrad when Saladin released King Guy of Jerusalem, who had been captured at Hattin in 1187. Upon his release, Guy and his brother, as well as his wife and co-ruler, Sibylla, went to Tyre and demanded that Conrad hand over control of the city. He refused, saying that Guy had forfeited his kingdom with his capture at Hattin. The matter of who should rule the Kingdom of Jerusalem was, according to Guy, a matter to be decided by European kings on their way to the Holy Land. An internecine struggle over the rightful successor to the throne arose. This provides an excellent example of the complex medieval culture of family alliances and the struggle for power.

The king of Jerusalem, Guy of Lusignan, and Queen Sibylla, along with the newly arrived Crusaders, went to Acre, where they put the city under siege. In the midst of the stalemate at Acre, Sibylla died on July 25, 1190. Conrad of Montferrat in Tyre, who had suffered greatly from the aggression of King Guy and Queen Sibylla, objected to the declaration that the heiress to the throne of Jerusalem was Isabella, a half-sister to Sibylla. She was married to the Crusader Humphrey IV of Toron, who occupied a castle in what is now Lebanon. Conrad, allying himself with some fractious courtiers, managed to have Isabella's marriage annulled, and he married her himself. It was in this way that Conrad claimed that he was the rightful king of Jerusalem.

After the fall of Acre, negotiations led to the confirmation that Guy was the rightful king of Jerusalem and that Conrad was to be his successor. This was overturned when it was decided to have a vote among the nobles on who should be king. The dispute centered on the allegiance of the two contenders for the throne. Guy was a vassal of Richard I, and Conrad was supported by his cousin, Leopold V of Austria, a cousin of King Philip II of France. In April of 1192, the barons elected Conrad as the king due to the support he had. To compensate Guy for his loss, Richard I sold him the lordship of Cyprus. He was motivated to do this to avoid having Guy return to Poitou in France where he would be likely to cause trouble in Richard's French domain.

Conrad of Montferrat, however, did not get the prize of being crowned as king of Jerusalem. While walking the streets of Tyre on April 28, 1192, he was stabbed by two Hashshashin, an order of assassins, and was mortally wounded. There was no shortage of suspects of who might have hired the assassins. Some say that it was

King Richard himself, others suspect the first husband of Isabella, Humphrey IV of Toron, and some even suggest that it was Saladin himself.

Baldwin IV, King of Jerusalem from 1174 to 1185, had left a will in which he stated that the most legitimate heir should rule as regent until the succession was settled by the kings of England, France, and the Holy Roman emperor. With the passing of Baldwin IV, who had inherited his throne from his father Amalric I, the Kingdom of Jerusalem passed to the underage Baldwin V, or Baldwin of Montferrat, Baldwin IV's nephew. After a reign of a little more than a year, he died in 1186. He was succeeded by Sibylla, one of two surviving children of Amalric.

Prior to her assumption of the throne, Sibylla had been the subject of intense negotiations for an appropriate spouse so she could produce an heir to the throne. Baldwin IV arranged for her to marry William Longsword of Montferrat, who was a cousin of the French king and the Holy Roman emperor. Less than a year into their marriage, William died. Sibylla managed to produce a son, though, whom she called Baldwin. The widow and the heir presumptive to the Kingdom of Jerusalem were seen as excellent prizes by Philip of Flanders, who demanded that she marry one of his vassals. His plan was rebuffed by the court. Other marital alliances were also proposed. Among them were the Crusader knights Baldwin of Ibelin, Guy of Lusignan, and Hugh III of Burgundy. Any of these alliances would have the benefit of ensuring European military support for the Kingdom of Jerusalem. Sibylla eventually married Guy with whom she co-ruled, producing for him two daughters.

King Richard I of England did not retake Jerusalem. He approached the Holy City two times but was forced to retreat. After being beaten back a second time by Saladin, Richard consulted with his most powerful nobles. The army council was divided. Most wanted to attack Saladin's base of power in Egypt, but the French knights led by the Duke of Burgundy wanted to attack Jerusalem. An abortive attack was made in the south against the Egyptians. This only further divided the contending nobles as to what to do. Richard, now ill and with a mind to return home, made a truce with Saladin on September 2, 1192. Saladin promised Christian pilgrims free access to Jerusalem and agreed to the leveling of his fortifications at Ashkelon.

Like most of the leaders of Crusader armies, Richard was always mindful of threats to his power at home. His brother, John, and King Philip II of France posed a constant danger to his control over his English and French lands. On October 9, 1192, Richard boarded a ship to take him back to Europe. His journey turned out to be even more perilous than remaining in the Holy Land, though. Due to storms, his vessel sought safety in the harbor of the island of Corfu. This put Richard in danger of being captured by the Byzantine emperor, Isaac II Angelos, who was displeased with Richard's conquest of Cyprus and his turning it over to one of his vassals. Richard escaped Corfu disguised as a Knight Templar, but the ship he was traveling on was wrecked near Aquileia, located at the head of the Adriatic Sea. Forced to travel overland, Richard and his troops were captured near Vienna shortly before Christmas by Leopold V, Duke of Austria. He charged Richard with complicity in the assassination of his brother-in-law, Conrad of Montferrat. When he was participating in the Crusade, Leopold suffered the indignity of having his role in the capture of Acre ignored by Richard. He had assumed command of the troops of the Holy Roman Empire on the death of Frederick Barbarossa and felt that he had equipped himself well in the siege and was thus due the same kind of authority as the kings of France and England. His banner was unceremoniously tossed over the city walls by Richard so that only those of the Kingdoms of Jerusalem, England, and France were flying on the ramparts of Acre.

Leopold's imprisonment of Richard the Lionheart was condemned by Pope Celestine III on the grounds that Crusaders performing God's duty were immune from secular authority. The Duke of Austria was thus excommunicated for his actions. Leopold relieved himself of his prisoner by turning him over to Holy Roman Emperor Henry VI. Henry himself had been, in his mind, betrayed by Richard. Specifically, his complaint involved the Plantagenet's support of the family of one of Henry's rebellious nobles, Henry the Lion of Saxony, and his loss of southern Italy to this one-time ally of Richard. Henry held Richard for ransom, hoping to get enough for him to finance an expedition to southern Italy to recoup lands lost to his empire, demanding an enormous sum for the release of the King of England. In response to this, the pope nearly excommunicated him. However, Richard's mother, Eleanor of Aquitaine, worked diligently to raise the ransom. The English were taxed, and the gold and silver of the churches were confiscated. While she was busy gathering the money, Henry received another offer. Richard's brother John and King Philip of France promised a more substantial sum if Henry would hold Richard until the fall of 1194. Henry rejected this offer and set Richard free on February 4, 1194.

While Richard was captive, his brother John revolted, and Philip of France invaded Richard's Duchy of Normandy. Upon his release, Richard hurried to his Norman lands and began a program of improving defenses. His primary construction was an enormous castle, the Château Gaillard, which began in 1196. Such a structure would normally take medieval masons at least ten years to build, but the costly fortifications were completed within two years. The speed of work on this building was a result of Richard's meticulous supervision of the construction. It is likely that Richard himself was the overall architect of Château Gaillard. It was an innovative structure with three perimeter walls enclosing dry moats. The inner keep and concentric walls were fitted with machicolations, or openings suspended outside the walls from which stones or boiling oil or water could be dropped on enemy troops at the base of the walls. This was one of the first uses of machicolations in Europe. Their appearance at Château Gaillard had been attributed to Richard's intense study of Muslim fort building in the Holy Land.

Richard's war against King Philip was supported by several allied nobles holding grudges against the French king. Richard's skill in negotiating with potential supporters was formidable, both while he was on Crusade and while he was securing his holdings in Normandy. In the latter venture, he was supplied with knights from the armies of Baldwin of Flanders and Renaud, Count of Boulogne. Until his death in 1194, Sancho VI of Navarre assisted by forcing Philip to deploy troops to fight him in the south. Richard won several victories over Philip. As was common at the time, a monarch spent a significant amount of time suppressing revolts among his dependent nobles. In one of these expeditions, Richard attacked Aimar V, Viscount of Limoges, and besieged his castle where it was rumored large caches of gold were stored. One evening, Richard, not wearing his chainmail, wandered at the foot of the castle walls, inspecting the work of his sappers. He was shot by a crossbow from above. The removal of the bolt was botched, and the wound became gangrenous. Richard died on April 6, 1199. He was succeeded by his brother King John, who lost almost all of the English lands in France to Philip II.

Chapter 6 – The Fourth Crusade (1202-1204) – The Latin Empire of Constantinople and the Children's Crusade (1212)

The failure of the Third Crusade to restore Jerusalem, the holiest of all Christian places on earth, to Christian control irked European ecclesiastics. First among them was Pope Innocent III, who had been elected to the highest church office in January 1198. He viewed Saladin's capture of Jerusalem in 1187 as a result of the moral degeneration of Christian princes. Because they were wanting in moral authority, Innocent III considered secular authorities unqualified to make appointments to ecclesiastical offices and entirely unjustified in meddling in Church affairs. Partly to emphasize his authority, Innocent III published a papal bull, *Post Miserabile*, in which he called for a new Crusade shortly after his election. He began by stating that the Muslims believed that they had "weakened and shattered the spears of the French" and that they had "crushed the efforts of the English." According to the pope, the Muslims were basking in their defeat of the Christians, saying that their victory was made possible because the Crusaders "prefer to fight each other in turn than to experience once more our might and power." The pope called for ecclesiastics to call for a renewal of the Crusading spirit, for Christians to renew their religious enthusiasm and pay attention "to how our enemies persecute us." Among the most successful in carrying the pope's message to the people was Fulk of Neuilly, a French cleric who persuaded Count Theobald III, Count of Champagne, to take the cross. Theobald was chosen as the first leader of the new Crusade, but he died in 1201. He was replaced as the primary leader of the Crusade by the Italian Boniface I, Marquess of Montferrat, whose father had been on the Second Crusade and whose brothers were William "Longsword," Count of Jaffa and Ascalon (also known as Ashkelon), and King Conrad of Jerusalem. Boniface, according to his friend and court poet, Raimbaut de Vaqueiras, had already engaged in knightly activities that merited the honor of being told about in lyrical ballads. He had rescued an heiress, Jaopina of Ventimiglia, whose uncle imprisoned her in an attempt to steal her inheritance. He also rode to the rescue of Saldina de Mar, the daughter of a Genoese merchant who had been abducted by Boniface's brother-in-law. Boniface kindly restored her to the arms of her lover. Clearly, Boniface of Montferrat had the qualities necessary for leading a Crusade.

When he called for the launch of the Fourth Crusade, Innocent received significant support in France. He funded the campaign by first levying a tax on the clergy, who were to render up one-fortieth of their income, and then cajoling the English monarch, King John, and King Philip II of France to pledge a similar amount of their income to the cause. King John also decided that this tax would be collected throughout his kingdom. This commitment was to have important repercussions on the extent of his power as king.

The first challenge faced by the leader of the Fourth Crusade was securing transport to Egypt, where it was intended to deal a blow against the predominant Muslim power in the east. An agreement was made with the city of Venice, which was led by the blind Doge Enrico Dandolo, to supply a fleet of ships sufficient enough to carry

4,500 knights and their horses, 9,000 squires, and 20,000 infantry soldiers across the Mediterranean. The convoy was to be protected by fifty fighting galleys. Such a large fleet required a year to prepare. New vessels were constructed in the Venetian shipyards, and crews were trained to man them. For their service, the Venetians were to be paid 94,000 marks.

In June of 1202, the fleet was ready, and the Crusaders were assembled to board. Unfortunately, the army of fighting men, most of them from France and Lombardy in northern Italy, fell far short of the amount that was to be paid to the Venetians. The promised payment to the Venetians, which was to be raised by charging each of the knights to travel on the ship, fell some 43,000 marks short of the goal. The Crusaders' predicament was recorded in a chronicle, *On the Conquest of Constantinople*, which was written by one of the Crusaders, Geoffrey of Villehardouin. "Every man in the army was called upon to pay the cost of his passage. A very considerable number said that they could not pay the full amount…The money collected did not amount of half, much less the whole, of the sum required." Unable to fulfill their contract with the Venetians, the nobles debated whether to borrow money or forfeit their deposits and return home. Several of the knights handed over what they had to the Venetians. "It was a marvel to see the many fine table-services of gold and silver plate borne to the Doge's palace to make up the payment due." The Doge of Venice, Enrico Dandolo, agreed to temporarily forgo the remaining debt, expecting to be paid back from the spoils of the Crusade. He also agreed to provide additional Venetian troops for the expedition.

One Sunday, the Venetians gathered at the Church of San Marco of Venice, and the Doge chose to address the Crusaders.

> You are associated with the best and bravest people in the world in the highest enterprise anyone has ever undertaken. Now I am an old man, weak and in need of rest, and my health is failing. All the same I realize that no one can control and direct you like myself, who am your lord. If you will

consent to my taking the cross so that I can protect and guide you…I shall go to live or die with you and with the pilgrims.

The Venetians and their leader were eager to join the Crusade because they planned to divert the army to Constantinople and restore Alexios IV Angelos, the son of Emperor Isaac II Angelos, to the Byzantine throne. The condition for support demanded by Dandolo, who became the real leader of the Crusade, was that the fleet make a detour on its journey to Egypt and deal with enemies of Venice. No mention was made of the ultimate goal of putting Alexios IV on the imperial throne in Constantinople.

On October 1, 1202, a fleet of more than 200 ships set sail from Venice for Zara, located on the Dalmatian coast in modern-day Croatia, as not enough money had been raised to send them to Egypt. Zara had rebelled against the Venetian Republic in 1183, making it a target that Dandolo found hard to resist. They began the siege on the city on November 13, and the city fell by November 24, with some of the Crusader leaders refusing to take part in the attack because Zara was a Christian city. This marked the first time the Crusaders attacked a Catholic city. Many of the Crusaders, however, sided with Dandolo, seeing this as a minor setback to the more glorious goal of obtaining Jerusalem. Pope Innocent III condemned any attacks on Christians, and in 1203, he excommunicated the entire Crusader army along with the Venetians, although he would later grant absolution to the army.

After the Siege of Zara, the Crusaders proceeded to sack the city. Squabbles arose over the spoils of the battle which the Venetians claimed as rightfully theirs.

Boniface of Montferrat had left the fleet before it sailed from Venice to visit his cousin, Philip of Swabia, King of Germany, who was married to a Byzantine princess, Irene Angelina. Under Philip's protection was the refugee Alexios IV Angelos, who claimed to be the rightful Byzantine emperor. Boniface of Montferrat and Alexios discussed the diversion of the Venetian fleet to Constantinople.

Alexios sent messengers to the Crusaders, making extravagant promises of assistance plus money to pay off their debt to the Venetians. The offer was good enough for the indebted Crusaders. They still held the Byzantines in contempt for their treachery during the three previous Crusades, as well as their massacre of Latin Christians some twenty years before, where as many as sixty thousand people were killed or forced to flee Constantinople. The Crusaders had more than enough motive to fight the Byzantines on behalf of Alexios.

While they were stalled in Zara due to winter storms, the Crusaders were apprised of the negotiations between their leader, Boniface of Montferrat, and the son of the deposed emperor of Byzantium, Alexios IV Angelos. During their meeting in Swabia, Montferrat accepted Prince Alexios' offer to pay the Crusaders a huge sum of silver marks, increase their number by the addition of 10,000 Byzantine soldiers, submit the Eastern Church to the authority of Rome, and supply a permanent contingent of Byzantine soldiers to secure the Holy Land. In return for this generous offer, the Venetians and the Crusaders agreed to overthrow the Byzantine emperor, Alexios III Angelos, and install Alexios. Hearing about this, Pope Innocent III issued an order forbidding any more attacks on Christians unless they were hindering the Crusader cause, but he never outrightly condemned this attack on Constantinople. He might have perhaps felt that the capture of Constantinople would be a way to reunite the Eastern and Western Churches once again.

Finally able to move on, the Venetian fleet, commanded by Doge Enrico Dandolo, arrived in the poorly defended harbor of Constantinople in late June 1203. They attacked and were repulsed from some of the suburbs of the city, so they planned a greater siege for the city itself. The siege started on July 11, but the real fighting didn't begin until July 17. On that day, the Venetians scaled the walls of Constantinople from the seaward side, and part of the Crusader army assembled for battle outside the walls on the landward side. The Byzantine army marched out of the city but quickly withdrew in the face of the superior Crusader army. Emperor Alexios III deserted the city, and the gates were thrown open, with Alexios IV Angelos being proclaimed emperor.

Alexios IV, finding the treasury of Byzantium depleted and unable to gain the support of his nobles and ecclesiastics who hated the interlopers from the Roman Church, was unable to raise sufficient funds to pay his debt to the Crusaders. His subjects objected to his promise to make the Eastern Church subservient to the Western Church, and they refused to serve in the Crusader army commanded by European nobles. In December 1203, war broke out between the disgruntled Byzantines and the Crusaders. In a palace coup in Constantinople toward the end of January 1204, Alexios was overthrown, and he was later strangled in prison on February 8, 1204, on the orders of the usurper Alexios V Doukas.

The Crusaders were now stranded outside Constantinople without the funds necessary to proceed to their goal in the Near East. The Venetians were angered over the fact that the financial rewards for their efforts on behalf of Alexios IV were not to be forthcoming. Montferrat's nobles and the Venetian merchants met to discuss their next course of action. Naturally, they concluded that even if the Byzantine treasury was depleted, there were sufficient treasures to be had within the city to justify a siege. In an attack on Constantinople on April 12, the Venetian galleys pulled up close enough to the city walls to disembark soldiers across flying bridges. The men proceeded to open the city gates, allowing a throng of mounted knights to enter. The next day, the resistance of the city's citizens evaporated with the departure of Alexios V Doukas and most of the Byzantine upper class. The Crusaders and Venetians proceeded to sack the city. It was, according to Villehardouin, "a city richer than any other since the beginning of time. As for the relics, these were beyond all description." They amassed some 900,000 marks worth of treasure. This was apportioned to knights and soldiers based on their rank. Some Crusaders were able to pay off their debt for the cost of their passage to the Venetians, but others were not.

During the following three days, the Crusaders looted the city and terrorized its remaining inhabitants, who had been abandoned by most of the nobility. The sack of Constantinople included the destruction or theft of many ancient and medieval artworks. Four bronze horses that decorated the Hippodrome were carted off by the Venetians to one of their galleys. These 4th-century BCE monumental sculptures were then shipped to Venice and installed over the porch of the San Marco Basilica, where they still stand today. The fate of the bronze horses was not the same as a huge bronze sculpture of Hercules, which could be dated to the 4th century BCE as well. It was toppled from its pedestal and melted down. The Crusaders, who lacked effective leadership, rampaged throughout the city. They not only destroyed the Library of Constantinople, which may have held around 100,000 manuscripts, but they also smashed and melted down the treasures in churches, monasteries, and convents. The Venetian army was more disciplined, and instead of destroying the treasures they found, they collected them and shipped them home. The gold coins acquired in the sack of the city were sufficient to pay the Crusaders' debt to the Venetians with plenty left over to be divided among all of the European knights.

Only a small handful of knights actually made it to the designated goal of the Holy Land. Pope Innocent III, after hearing the news of the destruction of Constantinople, strongly rebuked the knights but did not offer any punishment. In fact, he accepted the stolen treasures that were sent to him and recognized the new authority in the Byzantine Empire.

Now under the control of the Latins, as the Crusaders were called, Constantinople was put under the authority of a new emperor. The choice of the European invaders was Baldwin, Count of Flanders. Baldwin's brother-in-law Philip had married Baldwin's sister, Queen Isabella I of France. Baldwin, whose sister had died in 1190, had taken the cross after negotiating a treaty with his archenemy, the King of France Philip II Augustus, in 1200. He was noted for his piety and virtue, and his capacities as a leader were far superior to the nominal leader of the Crusade, Boniface of Montferrat. Baldwin was crowned emperor on May 16, 1204.

Baldwin's empire was organized as a European feudal state. Nobles were granted fiefdoms in conquered Byzantine territories. After the coronation of Baldwin, an alliance between the Bulgarians and the emperor was negotiated by Pope Innocent III. This was an effort to secure the frontiers of the Latin Empire of Constantinople. However, peace did not endure for long as the Crusaders made incursions into the territories under the control of the Bulgarian king or tsar, Kaloyan. He responded by breaking his alliance with Baldwin and allied Bulgaria with the Greeks in Thrace. In the spring of 1205, the citizens of Adrianople revolted against their Latin overlords. Baldwin led perhaps as few as 4,000 of his troops and Venetian fighters out of Constantinople and laid siege to the city of Adrianople. Kaloyan, after hearing of the siege, brought his army south from Bulgaria. His force consisted of 54,000 men. On April 14, 1205, Kaloyan drew Baldwin's army into an ambush, killing many knights and taking Baldwin prisoner. Baldwin died in prison around 1205 (it is unknown when he actually died because Kaloyan only claimed that Baldwin had without providing sufficient proof) in the medieval capital of Bulgaria, Veliko Tarnovo. The Venetians, having fulfilled their contract to defend Baldwin until the year 1205, boarded their vessels and sailed home.

Baldwin was succeeded in 1206 by his younger brother, Henry of Flanders, who had distinguished himself in the siege of Constantinople in 1204. Under his leadership, the Latin Empire of Constantinople expanded its control of Byzantine territories. These were ceded by Henry to important Crusader nobles. One of these was Boniface of Montferrat, who took his knights to the second-largest Byzantine city, Thessalonica, where, in spite of Pope Innocent III's instructions that the Crusaders not wage war against Christians, succeeded in taking the city from its Byzantine defenders. He assumed the title of King of Thessaly. Boniface continued his aggression, bringing most of Greece and Macedonia under his control. He was supported in his hostile actions against Byzantine Christians by Emperor Henry. The most successful opponent to the expansion of the Latin Empire of Constantinople was the Tsar of Bulgaria, Kaloyan. Montferrat's rule as King of Thessaly was cut short after two years when he was killed in battle with the Bulgarians on September 4, 1207.

According to historical records, Henry was a magnanimous emperor, even going so far as to enlist advisors and soldiers from among the Byzantine nobility of Constantinople. It was said that, even though a foreigner, he treated the people of the city as if they were his own. An example of this is his countermanding the orders of the papal legate, a personal representative of the pope, who had been sent to Constantinople with the purpose of imprisoning the Orthodox clergy and closing their churches.

Henry's reign came to an end with his death on June 11, 1216. There is no doubt that he was poisoned, but who murdered him or on whose orders it was carried out remains a matter of debate. Many think his second wife, Maria of Bulgaria, daughter of Bulgarian Tsar Kaloyan, had perpetrated the act.

Henry was succeeded by his brother-in-law, Peter II of Courtenay, who had participated in the Third Crusade and fought against enemies of the Church in France. He left his home in northern France and made his way with an entourage of knights to Rome where Pope Honorius III crowned him emperor of Constantinople on April 9, 1217. On his way to Constantinople to claim his empire, he was captured by the Byzantine ruler of Epirus, Theodore Komnenos Doukas. Peter of Courtenay died after two years of imprisonment.

When news of Peter's death reached France, his son, Robert of Courtenay, was declared emperor of Constantinople. On his way to assume leadership of the capital of the Latin Empire, he engaged in battle with Emperor Theodore Doukas of the Empire of Thessalonica, who had only tenuous control over bits and pieces of the empire in Europe. Robert's knights and foot soldiers were defeated, and his authority in Greece was usurped by Theodore Doukas. Robert also had to relinquish control over Anatolia to the so-called Byzantine Emperor of Nicaea, who was a second claimant to the Byzantine imperial throne, Theodore I Lascaris. In a dispute over his proposed marriage and thus succession to the imperial throne, Robert was driven from Constantinople by Burgundian knights. He fled to Rome to seek the assistance of the pope. On his return journey to Constantinople in 1228, he died.

Baldwin II, then an eleven-year-old, was proclaimed emperor under the regency of John of Brienne. Throughout his reign from 1228 to 1273, Baldwin II was constantly in search of money to support the defense of his empire, which consisted of little more than the city itself. He made the rounds of potential financiers in Europe in 1236 and achieved a measure of success. To raise money, he helped himself to the Crown of Thorns, which had been placed on Jesus' head before he was crucified. This had once belonged to the Byzantines but was later pawned to a Venetian merchant as security for a loan. It was taken from them to bring to Paris and was given to Louis IX in 1238. He built one of the jewels of Gothic architecture, the elegant Sainte-Chapelle, to house this relic. (After the French Revolution, the Crown of Thorns was deposited in Notre Dame Cathedral. It was one of the treasures of the cathedral saved by firemen in the conflagration of April 15, 2019.)

In spite of enlisting some soldiers and raising some badly needed funds, Baldwin was unable to defend Constantinople, and it was overrun by the Greeks on July 24, 1261, thus effectively ending the Latin Empire of Constantinople, although the title was still held until 1383. The Byzantines installed Michael VIII Palaeologus as emperor. Baldwin II escaped and subsequently lived in retirement in France.

Children's Crusade 1212

Because documentary evidence for the Children's Crusade has been considered more stuff of myth and legend than factual, it is not included in the sequential numbering of Christian expeditions to the East. Nevertheless, it is useful to consider this particular Crusade because it sheds light on the ethos of Christian Europe in the midst of the long and enduring passion for the Crusades.

The Children's Crusade, according to what records do exist on it, consisted of two waves. It was said that a German shepherd boy from Cologne, named Nicholas, preached a Crusade to receptive children. These, in turn, persuaded others to join them. Having gathered, a following of disciples, which according to some records may have numbered 21,000, were led across the Alps into Italy by Nicholas. The *Chronica regia Coloniensis,* or *Royal Chronicle of Cologne,* includes the following passage.

> Many thousands of boys, ranging in age from six years to full maturity, left the plows or carts they were driving, the flocks which they were pasturing, and anything else which they were doing. This they did despite the wishes of their parents, relatives, and friends who sought to make them draw back. Suddenly one ran after another to take the cross. Thus, by groups of twenty, or fifty, or a hundred, they put up banners and began to journey to Jerusalem. The children claimed that it was the will of the Divine that prompted them to undertake this Crusade. In spite of this, their expedition did not achieve its intention in the end.

On the journey south, particularly on the treacherous paths through the Alps, two-thirds of the Crusaders died. Their goal was Genoa where, said Nicholas, God would cause the sea to part and the Crusaders could then walk to the Holy Land. When this didn't happen, some turned on Nicholas, and some settled down to await the miraculous appearance of a dry passage to the East. The

Genoese, sympathetic to the stranded young Crusaders who were camped on their doorstep, offered them safe haven and absorbed their numbers into the urban population. Nicholas, undeterred by the failure of God to provide a dry path to the Holy Land, led a few of his remaining flock to Rome where they met with Pope Innocent III, who told them that they were too young to go to the East. Nicholas then disappears from historical records. He apparently perished on re-crossing the Alps.

A second wave of youth Crusaders formed in France around the charismatic twelve-year-old Stephen of Cloyes. He said that in a dream he had been given a letter from Christ addressed to the king of France. Stephen gathered 30,000 disciples; this number included some adults who were taken with the piety of the group and impressed by the mystical communion many of the children claimed to have with God. The Crusaders went to Saint-Denis to meet with the French king, Philip II. He was unimpressed by their cause and presumably told them to return to their homes. Undaunted, Stephen went to a nearby abbey and continued to preach his Crusade. As his throng journeyed south, their numbers depleted so that by the time they reached Marseille, perhaps half remained. Unable to find transport to the Holy Land, they disbanded, and those that did not return home were captured by unscrupulous merchants and sold into slavery.

In modern times, several historians have attempted to elicit the meaning of the story of the Children's Crusade. One has said that it represents "diseased religious emotionalism." Another source considers it to be an archetypical moral tale of innocents sacrificing themselves for their faith. Yet another has thought it to be a story of chivalric piety with an anti-war motif. It may, some have written, been a paean of the poor and the dispossessed seeking relief from their misery. A close reading of the texts about the Children's Crusade suggests that the participants were not all children but simply those who suffered under the drudgery of agricultural labor as the *Chronica regia Coloniensis*, written in 1213, suggests in the passage quoted above.

Chapter 7 – The Fifth Crusade (1217-1221)

The diversion of the Fourth Crusade to Constantinople was understood by many in the West as an example of Venetian treachery motivated by the greed of merchants to monopolize maritime trade in the East. Pope Innocent III was disappointed in the Fourth Crusade because it involved only battles with fellow Christians. The Crusaders had done nothing with respect to the removal of Muslims from the Holy Land.

Pope Innocent III had more than Muslim enemies on his mind after the end of the Fourth Crusade. In southern France, a heretical sect of Christians, the Cathars, also known as Albigensians after the town of Albi where the movement first took hold, had usurped the power of the Catholic Church. The Cathars, who believed in two deities, one good and the other evil, declared themselves independent of the authority of the Church, believing it to be thoroughly corrupt and doctrinally in error. The Cathars were, as well, proto-feminists. According to their faith, they held that both women and men could administer the holy sacraments. This was abhorrent to the patriarchal Catholic Church. The killing of his legate to the court of Count

Raymond VI of Toulouse in 1208 ended Innocent III's peaceful attempt to convince the Cathars of the errors of their beliefs. He excommunicated Count Raymond, who was not a Cathar himself, for being too lenient in his dealings with the heretical sect. In order to destroy the heretics by means of the sword, Innocent called on the French king, Philip II, to launch a Crusade against the heretics in the south of France. Neither Philip nor his son Louis joined in the expedition; however, many northern nobles rode off to Languedoc, having been promised that they could keep any of the lands that they might capture.

The Crusaders, under the command of the papal legate, the Abbot of Cîteaiux, in their first engagement with the Cathars, attacked the town of Béziers on July 22, 1209, where they massacred some 7,000 inhabitants, making little effort to distinguish between Cathars and Catholics. A long series of sieges and massacres followed, in which the so-called Albigensian Crusaders prevailed over the breakaway sect. The Cathars were subsequently hunted down and executed by the Inquisition, which was established in 1233.

The Crusade against the Cathars was not the only Crusade fought on European soil. In the Iberian Peninsula, the notion of a Crusade was invoked to hasten the removal of the Moors from Spanish and Portuguese lands. The ongoing struggle against the Muslims, or Moors, known as the Reconquista, began to turn in favor of the Christians in a Crusade called by Pope Innocent III. The coalition of monarchs and nobles from Spain and France joined Alfonso VIII, King of Castile, in opposing the Almohad Caliphate leaders from the southern half of the Iberian Peninsula. Under Caliph al-Nasir, an army of North African Muslims crossed the Strait of Gibraltar to firm up Muslim control of Al-Andalus (modern Andalusia). The huge Muslim force threatened to push north and dislodge the Christian forces who were firmly in control of about half of Spain. Alfonso VIII's coalition of French and Spanish nobles and monarchs attacked the Muslims. In the Battle of Las Navas de Tolosa, the Christians surprised the Moors and routed them on July 16, 1212.

Alfonso then pushed south toward Andalusia, where his army massacred and enslaved an enormous number of Muslims. Perhaps as many as 100,000 Muslims were captured, according to a contemporary chronicle of the campaign. After the Battle of Las Navas de Tolosa, the Spanish and their allies proceeded to slowly push the Moors out of the Iberian Peninsula. The Reconquista, which lasted 781 years, was completed with the surrender of Granada in 1492.

While the Crusade against the Albigensian heretics was unfolding and the Moors were losing ground in Spain, Innocent issued a papal bull in 1213 and another in 1215 calling for all in Christendom to support a new Crusade to rid the Holy Land of the Muslims. With the failure of the secular leadership of the Fourth Crusade to do anything to further this cause, Pope Innocent III intended to place a new Crusader army under the direct leadership of the Church. The Crusade was to commence in 1217.

The mouthpiece for the pope in France, Cardinal Robert of Courçon, was unsuccessful in convincing French nobles to take the cross. Many of the nobles were fully occupied with forcibly taking the lands of Languedoc in the south from the nobles sympathetic to the Albigensian cause. When Pope Innocent III died suddenly in July 1216, his successor, Pope Honorius III, took up managing the preparations for the Crusade. He committed money from the papal treasury for the massive undertaking and levied a tax on Church officials and all ecclesiastics to pay for the expedition to the Levant. Honorius identified the prime source for Crusaders as the Holy Roman Empire. In spite of continual pressure from the pope, the King of Germany, Frederick II, put off assembling an army and embarking for the Holy Land. He did send some contingents, but these were not of the size he promised.

The only nobles to meet the deadline for the departure of the Crusade were Duke Leopold VI of Austria, Otto I of Merania, and King Andrew II of Hungary. Their armies converged at Spalato (Split) in Dalmatia and boarded Venetian vessels for transport to

Acre. The number of fighting men, perhaps as many as 10,000 knights, was such that they had to be ferried in waves down the Adriatic and eastward across the Mediterranean. The plan to sail on from Acre to Egypt was delayed because King Andrew, who was ill, decided to return home to Hungary in January of 1218. This depleted the army of Crusaders to such an extent that it was decided to wait for reinforcements from Europe. When they eventually arrived, the Crusaders sailed to Damietta at the mouth of the Nile.

Encamped across the Nile from Damietta, the Crusaders launched several attacks against the tower of Damietta. They were driven off each time by the defenders under the command of Sultan Al-Kāmil, the fourth ruler of the Ayyubid dynasty in Egypt that had been founded by Saladin. The Crusaders then developed an ingenious solution to breaching the defenses of Damietta that consisted of 3 walls, 28 towers, and a moat. Using a design created by a Church official, Oliver of Paderborn, who also served as a chronicler of the Crusade, the Christian soldiers tied two ships together and erected a castle-like structure with a lofty flying bridge on them. The contraption was maneuvered next to the tower of Damietta. The siege of the tower had failed for nearly two months; however, in a single day, the siege engine captured the tower. Crusader reinforcements arrived at the end of September 1218. With them was the Spaniard Cardinal Pelagius of Albano, who assumed command of the operation.

In February 1219, Sultan Al-Kāmil, fearing the imminent success of the Crusaders in their siege, rode off from Damietta to modern-day Al Manṣūra farther up the Nile. He deserted his troops, who soon followed him, stealing out of the city. The Crusaders dithered and did not push their advantage, choosing to merely surround the city and wait. Sultan Al-Kāmil attempted to sue for peace, offering to turn over Jerusalem and the surrounding territory if the Crusaders pulled out of Egypt. Cardinal Pelagius refused this offer, doing so again when the Muslims offered to sweeten the deal with a substantial cash payment. Pelagius' intransigence was foolish as the

Crusader camp was diminishing on account of some nobles and their entourages departing for home. He also refused to understand that the Muslim forces were on the verge of receiving reinforcements from troops as far away as Syria.

In the midst of the protracted negotiations at Damietta, an Italian monk, Francis of Assisi, the founder of the Franciscan order, arrived at the Crusaders' camp. His journey from the headquarters of his rapidly expanding order was one of several he undertook to preach the gospel. His intention in appearing at Damietta was to convert the Sultan of Egypt or become a martyr in the attempt. In an interim in the back and forth skirmishes between the Christians and Muslims, Francis, along with a fellow brother, made his way into the sultan's camp. According to the earliest biographies of Francis, he was well received but failed to shake either the sultan's or his advisors' belief in the Quran. Francis left the Crusaders' camp and sailed off to Acre and then to Italy.

In April of 1219, the Crusaders' camp was attacked by strengthened Muslim forces. The Crusaders held them off, and Pelagius then decided to reactivate the siege of Damietta. The determined attack failed, and it was followed by a Muslim ambush of Crusaders in which as many as 4,300 Crusaders were killed. At this point, the Egyptians attempted to negotiate another peace treaty. While it was under discussion in the Crusaders' camp, a vulnerability in the walls of Damietta was discovered by chance. The Crusaders swarmed up ladders and took the city without opposition. The siege of Damietta resulted in the deaths of at least 50,000 people due to lack of supplies and disease. Pelagius, a demanding and thoroughly unsympathetic leader, alienated the leaders of his own army, who disliked his style and objected to his tactics. In the spring of 1220, John of Brienne, the King of Jerusalem, left Damietta for Acre with his troops, and several Crusaders opted to return home to Europe. The depletion of Crusader forces was compensated by the arrival of contingents of Italian troops led by bishops and archbishops who were all inept commanders.

Throughout the rest of the year, the Crusaders settled into life in Damietta while the Egyptians reinforced their fortifications at Al Manṣūra. With the return of King John of Jerusalem and the arrival of German Crusaders, Pelagius commanded the Crusaders to attack Al Manṣūra. His troops marched south along the banks of the Nile, and they were followed by a fleet of some 600 ships and galleys that sailed up the river. In preparation for a siege of the well-fortified city, the Crusaders set up camp. Pelagius, who was completely lacking in tactical abilities, did not blockade Al Manṣūra, and the Muslim forces in the fort were, essentially, reinforced by Muslim forces from Syria who camped in a location that blocked any possibility of retreat by land from the Crusaders. The Egyptians set traps on the Nile and destroyed the Crusader supply ships. When Pelagius finally understood the danger the Crusaders were in, he ordered a retreat to Damietta. It was a complete fiasco. The Muslims destroyed dikes, flooding the only overland route north. Trapped and lacking supplies, the Crusaders were forced to negotiate an armistice on August 28, 1221. Muslim control over Jerusalem was not relinquished, so Innocent's idea of putting a Crusade under the command of men from the Church proved to be a complete disaster.

Chapter 8 – The Sixth Crusade (1228-1229) – The Holy Roman Emperor Frederick II Takes the Cross

The most powerful ruler in Europe in the first half of the 13th century was Frederick II, Emperor of the Holy Roman Empire. The son of Emperor Henry VI, Frederick was elected King of the Germans in 1196 at the age of two and was appointed King of Sicily at the age of three. His mother, Constance, ruled Sicily as regent, and after her death in 1198, Frederick came under the guardianship of Pope Innocent III. Before he reached the age of majority, Frederick's Kingdom of Sicily had dissolved into a number of independent principalities whose barons and adventurers had usurped imperial authority. Frederick had a similar problem in Germany, where, even after he was crowned as king in 1212, he had to share power with a rival king of Germany, Otto IV. After Otto's death in 1218, Frederick struggled to firm up support among the German nobility, and it was not until 1220 that he was crowned Holy Roman emperor by Pope Honorius III. Frederick spent the first part of his reign in Sicily where he consolidated his hold over the state through the promulgation of the Constitutions of Melfi in 1231. These laws ensured the primacy of written law over local traditions and ensured that Frederick held sway as an absolute monarch.

In 1225, Frederick II married Isabella II, the daughter of John of Brienne, King of Jerusalem. Now free from consolidating his power over his lands in Germany and Italy and with a significant matrimonial alliance that gave him some claim to power in the Holy Land, the emperor assembled his army in Brindisi, Italy. Shortly after they had embarked on their vessels in August of 1227, Frederick's troops began to die from an epidemic disease. The flotilla returned to Brindisi, at which point Pope Gregory IX excommunicated him for his failure to carry out his vow to go on Crusade. The pope had other reasons for punishing Frederick, as the emperor had for many years neglected his duty to the Church by forcefully attempting to expropriate papal lands in Italy.

Frederick ignored his excommunication and set off again for Acre in 1228. On the way, he diverted his fleet to Cyprus. He claimed the island as a fiefdom that had owed homage to the Holy Roman emperor since its capture by Richard the Lionheart during the Third Crusade. He demanded that the regent of Cyprus, John Ibelin, who also was called the Old Lord of Beirut, vacate his authority over Cyprus and Beirut.

Having secured his authority over Cyprus, Frederick sailed to Acre. On his arrival, he found the inhabitants of the city, now the nominal capital of the Kingdom of Jerusalem, to be hostile to his presence. The patriarch, the leader of the Eastern Church, and the clergy, knowing that he had been excommunicated, refused to support his Crusade. The nobles were reluctant to follow his orders, fearing that they would be obliged to make their fiefdoms in Syria dependencies of the Holy Roman emperor. They also held it against Frederick that he had demanded John Ibelin to forfeit his suzerainty over Beirut, the capital of modern-day Lebanon.

The forfeiture of local authority, that is paying homage to a king, prince, or other noble, was a serious matter for the Crusaders who had settled in the Near East. They had much more at stake than mere power. They had settled into a life that paralleled a noble's environment in Europe and benefited from the income provided by their appropriated domains abroad. For example, John Ibelin, in rebuilding Beirut after Saladin's conquest of the city, had erected a grandiose family palace in which he could luxuriate in fabulous surroundings. It was described by a visitor in 1212. The central hall had a pavement "made of marble, which imitates water moved by a light breeze. And this is done so subtly that whoever treads on it feels as if he were wading, marvelling at not leaving any impression of the depicted sand." They had "a fountain with a dragon as the centre-piece stood in the central hall, its jets cooling the air and the murmur of the water giving an altogether soothing effect." The ceiling was painted with a fresco representing the heavens, "with such life-like colours that clouds pass across, the west wind blows, and there the sun seems to mark out the year and the months, the days and the weeks, the hours and the moments by its movement in the zodiac." It is little wonder, having established himself and his court in such magnificent surroundings, that John Ibelin would have feared Frederick's designs on annexing the Holy Land into the Holy Roman Empire. If he were forced to pay homage to Frederick, he would be required to turn over a portion of his income to his superior.

Frederick's army, which was too small to engage with the forces of Sultan Al-Kāmil of Egypt, could only hope for success on his mission by means of negotiation. Fortunately, the sultan was preoccupied with the suppression of rebels in Syria, so he consented to Frederick's terms in a treaty signed on February 18, 1229. In the treaty, he agreed to cede Jerusalem to the Christians along with the important pilgrimage cities of Nazareth and Bethlehem and the cities of Sidon and Jaffa. The Muslims did not turn over control of the

Temple Mount, al-Aqsa Mosque, and the Dome of the Rock in Jerusalem. The truce enacted by the treaty was to last ten years.

Frederick, basking in the glory of his diplomatic coup, made a triumphal entry into Jerusalem on March 17, 1229. He proceeded to have himself crowned as King of Jerusalem. In fact, he obtained authority only as regent acting in place of his son, Conrad, who was the heir to the throne of Jerusalem through his mother Isabella II. The Latin Patriarch of Jerusalem, Gerold of Lausanne, who adamantly refused to bow to Frederick's authority, did not preside over the so-called coronation. On the next day, the Latin Patriarch placed the city under an interdict, which is a ban that prohibits people from participating in certain rites.

In May 1229, Frederick left Jerusalem and sailed back to Europe. Although his Crusade involved no battles, he had proved to the European monarchs who were to follow in his footsteps that adventuring in the Holy Land did not require papal authority. His was a purely secular mission.

The nobles and clergy of the Kingdom of Jerusalem refused to accept the departed Frederick's assumption of the kingdom into his empire. The barons, among whom was John Ibelin, who was still smarting over his treatment in Cyprus, was one of those who resisted the representatives of the now-departed Holy Roman emperor. Frederick's viceroy was forced out of Acre within months.

After returning to Europe, Frederick had his excommunication lifted in the Treaty of Ceprano, which was signed in August of 1230. More important was the agreement between Frederick II and Pope Gregory IX to cease hostilities over territories claimed by the papacy.

Chapter 9 – The Seventh Crusade (1248-1254)

The peace brokered by Frederick in the Holy Land ended when Jerusalem was attacked by an army of Khwarezmians. These Sunni Muslim Turks had been forced out of their lands in Central Asia and Iran by invading Mongols. In the face of the collapse of their empire, the Khwarezmians moved south, seeking an alliance with Egyptian Mamluks. On the way, they laid siege to Jerusalem and occupied it in August 1244. They killed all but 2,000 of the inhabitants who remained in the city, leveling their defenses and buildings.

While the European Christians were simultaneously winning Spain and losing the Holy Land, a new scourge to security arose in the east. The enormous empire founded by the Mongol Genghis Khan and expanded by his sons and grandsons after his death in 1227 stretched from the Pacific Ocean to the shores of the Black Sea. Their westernmost conquests included Georgia, the Crimea, and Kievan Rus. These territories were the spoils of Batu Khan, a Mongol ruler and founder of the Golden Horde. The Mongols defeated the Kievan Rus nobles one by one, including the ruler of the principality of Vladimir-Suzdal, which included Moscow. The safety of the territory was guaranteed by the turning over of a young prince, Alexander Yaroslavich, to Batu as a hostage. Young Alexander absorbed the culture of the court of the Golden Horde, married a daughter of Batu Khan, and was placed as a Mongol prince in Novgorod where he defended the Mongols from the Swedes and the Germans. In the Battle of the Neva in July 1240, he trounced the Swedes, and for his military skill, he was given the sobriquet "Nevsky." Less than two years later, he repelled another invasion, this time a combined German-Latvian force who was routed in the Battle of the Ice. While Nevsky was thriving as a surrogate Mongol warrior, Batu laid siege to Kiev in December 1240. He then moved on into Poland, Hungary, and Transylvania and south into Croatia. The Mongols planned to follow up on their successes with an all-out attack on Germany, Austria, and Italy. In anticipation of his future military success in Europe, Batu demanded that Holy Roman Emperor Frederick II resign. The Mongol threat was sufficient for Pope Gregory IX to call for a Crusade against them. Central Europe escaped the Mongol invasion as the scourge from the East withdrew in 1242 to deal with issues of succession.

The Crusaders had a complicated relationship with the Mongols in the Levant. First, they allowed the Mamluks to move unhindered along their territory to defeat the Mongols at the Battle of Ain Jalut in 1260. But the Europeans soon changed tactics and enlisted the Mongols as allies in their fight against the Muslims. In the process of forming an alliance, the pope wrote to Mongol leaders encouraging them to convert to Western Christianity. This was not a completely unrealistic idea since a number of Mongols in the court were Nestorian Christians, members of a heretical Early Christian sect that had survived in the Persian Empire and the various Muslim dynasties that ruled the Persian Plateau, which was now entirely in the hands of the Mongols. A civil war in the Mongol Empire put an end to their abilities to fight as allies of the Christians.

In the Middle Ages, Europeans were fascinated with their co-religionist, albeit heretical, Nestorians and with the Mongols. A forged letter said to have been written to Byzantine Emperor Manuel

I Komnenos in the 12th century by Prester John, a legendary elder of an early Christian group called the Nestorians who, it was said, disappeared in India. The letter told of the wonders of the East and Nestorian Christianity. The legend of Prester John was so ingrained into the minds of Europeans that it was held that a descendant of Prester John, King David of India, was headed to the Kingdom of Jerusalem and that he would relieve it from the Muslim threat. The confusion between a supposed Asian Christian nation and the very real Mongols existed. Prester John became identified with Genghis Khan's foster father, Toghrul, and he was also attributed to have extraordinary powers. The myth was in large part deflated with the reports of European travelers, such as the Franciscan brothers, Giovanni da Pian del Carpine and William of Rubruck, who both visited the court of the Great Khan at Karakorum. Carpine's book *Ystoria Mongalorum* written in the 1240s, the oldest of European accounts of the Mongols, was followed by Rubruck's account, which he presented to Louis IX in 1253. An even more detailed description of the wonders of the East was written by Marco Polo, who spent 24 years traveling in Asia with his father and uncle. After his return home, Marco Polo, while in service with the Venetians in their conflict with Genoa, was captured at sea and imprisoned. He dictated the account of his adventures in the East to his fellow inmate, Rustichello da Pisa, an Italian writer of romances. Marco Polo's *Travels* was copied over and over again in manuscript form and was read widely throughout Europe from the 14th century on.

With inaccurate information on the Mongols spreading across the lands, the Europeans began to fear them as much as the Muslims in the Levant. A pleading missive for reinforcements went out from the few remaining Christian cities in the Holy Land. The loss of Jerusalem to the Khwarezmians in 1244 and the potential outcome of the Mongols overrunning the Holy Land indicated that without immediate aid, the Christian presence in the Holy Land would be in great jeopardy. Fortunately, King Louis IX of France, commonly known as Saint Louis, had already taken the cross. Louis convened a group of his nobles in Paris in October 1245. Most agreed to follow him on the overseas venture, and he imposed a substantial tax to pay for the Crusade.

Recognizing that the only way to save the Holy Land was to destroy the Egyptians, Louis, his knights, and fighting men set sail in 1248, wintering in Cyprus. After receiving a desperate request for aid from Bohemond V, Prince of Antioch, Louis dispatched 500 knights to help in defense of the Christian principality.

In May, Louis and his remaining force, which numbered about 2,700 knights, 5,000 crossbowmen, and 7,300 foot soldiers, sailed from Cyprus to Damietta. Landing on the beach, the Crusaders were attacked by Muslims, but their discipline held, and they forced the Egyptians to retreat and give up their outpost at Damietta. It was Louis' plan to spend the summer taking the fortified city, but the quick victory required him to reschedule his invasion as he did not want to move up the Nile until the flood season was over. Louis was one who learned from other's mistakes, and he was well aware that Pelagius had been stranded by the flooding Nile. To avoid the same fate, he settled down to await the end of summer. This itself was a risky undertaking. Fighting men tended to turn on each other in the absence of enemies. Disease was also rampant in crowded camps, and Crusader forces were always prone to losing men due to the departure of those who became disheartened, homesick, or ill.

In November, Louis led his troops south, moving up the Nile on the bank opposite the fortress at modern-day Al Manṣūra. When it came time to cross the Nile, the Crusaders were unable to construct an adequate bridge. Having been shown the location of a ford by a local Coptic Christian, they proceeded into the river. Many knights drowned in the crossing. Troops in the vanguard, under the command of Louis IX's brother, Robert of Artois, along with a contingent of Knights Templar and soldiers from England under Sir William Longespée (an illegitimate grandson of King Henry II), attacked the Egyptian camp a few kilometers from Al Manṣūra. The commanders of the Mamluk Turks, who were fighting alongside the forces of the Ayyubid sultan of Egypt, took command of the entire army defending the Nile Delta. Under their leaders, Faris ad-Din Aktai and Baibars al-Bunduqdari, they held off the Crusaders.

A picture of the kind of fighting that took place around Al Manṣūra is given by Jean of Joinville in his description of the Crusade in his *Life of Saint Louis*. The Crusader noble wrote that some 6,000 Turks attacked him and his knights.

> As soon as they saw us they came charging toward us, and killed Hugues de Trichâtel, Lord of Conflans, who was with me bearing a banner. I and my knights spurred on our horses and went to the rescue of Raoul de Wanou, another of my company, whom they had struck to the ground. As I was coming back, the Turks thrust at me with their lances. Under the weight of their attack my horse was brought to its knees, and I went flying forward over its ears. I got up as soon as ever I could, with my shield at my neck and sword in hand.

According to Joinville, his troops in retreating to a ruined house to await reinforcements were overrun. "A great body of Turks came rushing at us, bearing me to the ground and riding over my body, so that my shield went flying from my neck." When the Crusaders had scuttled into the house, the Turks struck again.

> Some of them got into the house and pricked us with their lances from above. My knights asked me to hold on to their horses' bridles, which I did, for fear the beasts should run away. Then they put up a vigorous defence against the Turks, for which, I may say, they were afterwards highly praised.

During this incident, some of the Crusaders suffered serious wounds that Joinville described in detail. Frédérick de Loupe had a lance thrust between his shoulders, which made "so large a wound that the blood poured from his body as if from the bung-hole of a barrel." A blow from one of the enemy's swords landed in the middle of Érard de Siverey's face, cutting through his nose so that it was left dangling over his lips.

The few remaining Crusaders from the vanguard escaped to join Louis, who was encamped nearby. There, the Crusaders managed to fight off several Muslim attacks. In the standoff, Louis opened negotiations with his enemy, offering to trade Damietta for Jerusalem. As talks dragged on, conditions deteriorated in the Christians' camp. The Muslims, as they had done in the past, prevented supply boats from traveling up from Damietta. Disease and declining morale forced the Crusaders to evacuate. The dangers of sailing, riding, or walking down the Nile through Muslim territory proved deadly. Crusader ships were attacked, and the stragglers on land were killed, as were the sick and diseased in the transport vessels. In the final battle of the Seventh Crusade at the Battle of Fariskur on April 6, 1250, the French were overwhelmed. Many of the prisoners that were too weak to walk were killed outright, and some of the defeated knights who were healthy were offered the, almost cliched, choice between death or conversion to Islam. Louis IX himself was captured along with his two brothers, Count Charles of Anjou and Count Alphonse of Poitiers. They were imprisoned in the house of the Egyptian royal chancellor at Al Manṣūra. Louis IX's brothers were eventually released and sent to France to secure the funds for a huge ransom for the king that was demanded by the Egyptians. Louis IX himself was tied in chains and shorn of his hair.

In France, there was, according to some with special affection for Louis IX, insufficient interest in raising his ransom. One of the outpourings of support came from a group of peasants; they were followers of an old Hungarian monk who they called the Master. He claimed to have been told by the Virgin Mary to enlist shepherds to join him in a mission to rescue the king. His Shepherds' Crusade of 1251 was said to have included 60,000 young men and women from Flanders and northern France. The enormous throng descended on Paris, where they entreated the regent Queen Blanche of Castile, Louis IX's mother, to support their cause. A contemporary ecclesiastical writer, Matthew Paris, viewed the Master as an imposter and that he was really one of the leaders of the Children's

Crusade of 1212. Having no effect on the royal household, the shepherds rampaged throughout the north of France, causing serious harm, attacking priests and monasteries and even expelling the Archbishop of Rouen and attacking Jews in Amiens and Bourges. They were, in time, rounded up and excommunicated, and the Master was killed in a fight near Bourges.

While the Shepherds' Crusade was going on, the Knights Templar arranged for a sum of 400,000 dinars to be transported to Egypt, thus paying Louis IX's ransom. The French king on his release sailed to Acre. His arrival there was described by Joinville. "All the clergy and the people of that city came down to the sea-shore in procession, to meet him and welcome him with very great rejoicing." King Louis spent four years there using monies from his treasury to rebuild the defenses of Acre, Caesarea, and Jaffa. In the spring of 1254, he and his army returned to France. When he went home in 1254, he left behind well-manned garrisons which he himself financed from the annual royal income.

The defeat of the French Crusaders at Al Manṣūra was principally owing to the military skill of Baibars al-Bunduqdari. He was a Mamluk Turk in service of Sultan Turanshah of Egypt, who was the great-great nephew of Saladin. After the defeat of the French, the Ayyubid sultan, who had come from Cairo, mistreated his faithful Mamluk soldiers and their leaders. The Mamluks revolted and killed the sultan.

Baibars, having proved himself to be an exemplary military leader in Egypt, marched with his army north to join a rival Mamluk warrior, Saif ad-Din Qutuz, in confronting the Mongols. The Mongols, who in their expansionist move to take over the world had sacked Baghdad and were now moving westward, had captured Aleppo and Damascus and threatened to attack Egypt itself. In the Battle of Ain Jalut in September of 1260 on the plains south of Nazareth, Qutuz and Baibars routed the Mongols. The Mamluks then retook Damascus and other Syrian cities. Qutuz did not get to savor his victory for, on his return to Cairo, he was assassinated. Baibars became the fourth in the Mamluk dynasty of sultans of Egypt.

Having put down an attempt to reinstate the Ayyubid rule in Cairo, Baibars then dealt with a fellow Mamluk, Emir Sinjar al-Halabi, who had occupied Damascus. After defeating him, Sultan Baibars turned to restore Egyptian control of Syria.

In 1263, Baibars attacked the city of Acre, the nominal capital of the Kingdom of Jerusalem. He was unsuccessful, so he turned to Nazareth. Using siege engines, the favored military machine of the Crusaders, his army breached the walls. He raised the citadel of Nazareth, and when he captured Haifa, he did the same. Afterward, Baibars besieged Arsuf. Baibars offered to release the captured Knights Hospitallerss if they agreed to abandon the city. They opted to accept the offer, but Baibars reneged and captured them. Baibars continued his successful invasion of the Levant. He forced the surrender of Antioch, razing the city, massacring much of population, and selling the remaining people into slavery. At Jaffa, he repeated the process as he did subsequently at Ashkelon and Caesarea.

Chapter 10 – The Eighth Crusade (1270)

The successes of Baibars in the 1260s in the Holy Land rightly alarmed the Europeans to such an extent that the King of France, Louis IX, then in his fifties, decided to launch another Crusade. He formally took the cross on March 24, 1267. Louis and his army set sail from the Provence port of Aigues-Mortes in the summer of 1270. His departure had been preceded by a Spanish contingent that departed from Barcelona under King James I of Aragon in the fall of 1269. The Aragonese flotilla was damaged by a storm, and most of the survivors returned to Spain, but a small contingent did struggle to Acre where they engaged with Baibars' troops. Unable to dislodge the Egyptian sultan, they returned home.

Louis IX abandoned his initial plan to sail to Cyprus and then on to the Holy Land. Instead, he chose to sail south to Tunis in North Africa, where he hoped to subdue the city by converting the caliph to Christianity and thus interrupt the forwarding of supplies to Egypt, weakening Baibars' sultanate.

Louis' forces were augmented by one provided by the King of Navarre, which sailed from Marseille. Both met off Sardinia and then proceeded to the coast of Tunisia. The arrival of the English fleet carrying Crusaders was delayed as Henry III of England, who had agreed to participate, backed out and sent his son Prince Edward instead.

After reaching North Africa, the Crusaders set up camp near Carthage. While awaiting reinforcements, they fell victim to a virulent epidemic of dysentery. Louis himself died of the disease on August 25, 1270. The Crusaders, after making a treaty with the caliph of Tunis, prepared to evacuate from North Africa. While most of the French troops returned home, Prince Edward of England took his army of about 1,000 men, including 225 knights, to Acre, where he disembarked on May 9, 1271.

The Ninth Crusade (1271–1272)

This Crusade is sometimes considered to be a part of the Eighth Crusade (which is why it does not have its own chapter), and it is commonly seen as the last Crusade to reach the Holy Land before the fall of Acre in 1291.

Hearing of the failure of Louis IX's Crusade in North Africa and the death of the king himself, the Mamluk Sultan Baibars rescinded his orders to his generals in Cairo to march westward to relieve Tunis. He continued to lay siege to Crusader castles in Syria during this time. At the seemingly impregnable Krak des Chevaliers, Baibars' army breached the outer walls in two days. They did this by using mangonels modeled after those of the Crusaders. Baibars then concocted a clever plan to force the defenders to surrender by sending them a forged letter. Purported to be from the Grand Master of the Knights Hospitallers, the letter instructed the Hospitallers stationed there to surrender. After a lull in fighting that lasted ten days, the Hospitallers, in early April 1271, negotiated their departure from Krak des Chevaliers, and their lives were spared.

The loss of Krak des Chevaliers was a blow to the Hospitallers. It was believed that the enormous castle was impregnable, and it had been the finest and largest of the Hospitallers' castles along the border of the County of Tripoli. In the mid-13th century, this outpost was defended by about 2,000 troops. The castle was surrounded by two concentric walls, and the three-meter-thick inner wall had seven protective towers, each ten meters in diameter. The castle was supplied with an enormous storeroom containing food sufficient enough to sustain the defenders throughout a siege of five years. The stable held as many as 1,000 horses.

In 1271, Prince Edward assessed the situation from Acre, the last remaining Christian stronghold in the Holy Land. With insufficient forces to fend off an attack by Baibars, he sent an embassy to the Mongols to enlist their help. This they provided by attacking Baibars' city of Aleppo, distracting him for a while. With Baibars busy at Aleppo, Edward attempted to open up a route to Jerusalem. However, he failed in this endeavor. In May of 1272, Hugh III of Cyprus, the King of Jerusalem, signed a ten-year truce with Baibars in an attempt to alleviate pressure on Acre, thus ending the Ninth Crusade.

Prince Edward's Crusader career ended when he was attacked by a Muslim assassin. The heir to the throne of England killed his assailant but suffered a severe stab wound in his arm. He survived thanks to the ministrations of his wife, Eleanor of Castile, who had accompanied him on his Crusade. In poor health, Edward left Acre on September 24, 1272, sailing to Sicily, where he learned that his father, Henry III, had died in November 1272. Edward put off returning to England, and eventually, he moved with his courtly entourage north, stopping in Italy and France where he met with Pope Gregory X in the summer of 1274. He arrived in England on August 2, 1274, and was crowned two weeks later. Informed of the dire situation in the Holy Land, Pope Gregory X attempted to raise enthusiasm in Europe for another Crusade but it fell on deaf ears, possibly because the papacy had, for many years, used the call for a Crusade to deal with European enemies, both secular and religious, rather than the Muslims in the Holy Land. With no reinforcements on the horizon, the King of Jerusalem, Hugh III, moved his court to

Cyprus in 1276. Although Baibars died in Damascus in July 1277, his successors continued to exert extreme pressure on the remaining Christian holdings in the Near East.

As the situation became even more dire in the Holy Land, Pope Nicholas IV, in 1289, tried in vain to inspire European kings and nobles to take the cross. His pleadings were unsuccessful as domestic conflicts distracted potential leaders of a Crusade.

In 1291, tensions around Acre, the last Crusader city in the Holy Land, came to a boil. A flotilla of Venetian galleys arrived with some 1,600 men. They were, according to some sources, ill-trained peasants and unemployed men from Tuscany and Lombardy. Upon disembarking, they attacked the Muslims in the vicinity of Acre. The Mamluk Sultan Al-Mansur Qalawun accused the Crusaders of breaching the treaty. He began mobilizing his forces for an all-out siege of Acre. Crusader peace negotiators sent to Cairo were ignored and imprisoned. Qalawun's son, who had succeeded his father as Mamluk sultan of Egypt and Syria, marched against the Crusaders. He was reinforced by fighters from Damascus and other towns and cities in the Levant, as well as a large contingent of soldiers from Cairo who arrived at Acre on April 6, 1291. Over a period of several days, the Muslims succeeded in undermining the walls of the city while they rebuffed Crusader attempts to negotiate a peace. On May 18, the Muslims launched an all-out attack against the now breachable walls. Street fighting reduced the number of Christian defenders, and eventually, those that were still alive evacuated the city and fled on galleys to Cyprus.

The fall of Acre in 1291 signaled the end of Christian Crusading activities in the Holy Land.

Conclusion

The Aftermath: The Idea of Crusading Continues

In August of 1308, Pope Clement V called for faithful Christians to take the cross for another Crusade to be launched the following year. The pope's plan was for the Hospitallers to lead a limited expedition to the East. He asked that those who preached the Crusade ask for prayers from the laity and the donation of funds to support the Hospitallers. In exchange for financing the Crusade, the pope, following in the steps of his predecessors, offered donors indulgences, or advance absolution for their sins.

Those who preached the Crusade were remarkably successful in stirring up the peasantry. Although the lower classes were not, in fact, encouraged to take the cross, many of them in Northern Europe proceeded to sew a red cross on their garb, assemble en masse, and hasten off to the papal palace at Avignon to offer their service to the pope. These poor Crusaders, who styled themselves as the "Brothers of the Cross," supported themselves on their journey south by attacking Jewish communities they met along the way and looting their property. In Brabant, Jewish people took refuge in the castle of Duke John II. They were saved when he sent his army out to chase the poor Crusaders away.

In July 1309, the poor Crusaders, possibly as many as 40,000, arrived in Avignon and asked the pope to authorize a full-scale Crusade. He refused, and the Hospitallers refused to board any of them on the ships that the peasants believed would take them to the Holy Land. Without papal authorization and without transport, the poor Crusaders dispersed and returned to their homes.

In the spring of 1311, a fleet of galleys in Brindisi was prepared for the Hospitallers. They set out on an expedition to the East, which they called a Crusade. The ships, carrying from 200 to 300 knights and 3,000 foot soldiers, landed on the Greek island of Rhodes. It was, in fact, never the intention of the Hospitallers to proceed to the Holy Land. Their goal was to complete the conquest of the island and remove the last Byzantine soldiers from the city of Rhodes. The Crusade was thus not directed at Muslims but fellow Christians. On August 15, 1311, the Hospitallers captured the city of Rhodes. The order then transferred its convent and hospital from Cyprus to Rhodes and commenced operations against Venetian trading posts in the Aegean Sea, as well as engaging with the Turkish fleet. In a naval battle in 1319 near the island of Chios, the Hospitallers defeated the Turks and set in motion a push to end Muslim seaborne predation in the Aegean.

The idea of launching military expeditions under the cover of the word "Crusade" was slow to die out. The King of Cyprus, Peter I, who was nominally King of Jerusalem—a kingdom without any territory in the Holy Land—spent three years from 1362 to 1365 forming an army and soliciting financial support for a Crusade. His venture, under the guise of a religious operation, appears to have been motivated by economics, more specifically the termination of Alexandria's primacy as a trading port, rather than religious fervor.

In October 1365, Peter's forces sailed to Rhodes where they picked up some Hospitallers. With 165 ships, he then sailed to Alexandria, and on October 9, 1365, he launched a vicious attack on the city. The massacre of the population and the leveling of buildings was followed by a withdrawal so Peter could proceed farther into Egypt.

His plan was cut short when the knights in his army refused to continue with the invasion, preferring to return home with their loot.

The gradual corruption of the notion of a Crusade is clear in the several so-called Crusades that were launched in Europe over the centuries following the fall of Acre in 1291. An example of this is the Crusade launched by Pope Urban VI against the supporters of the antipope in Avignon, Clement VII, who was elected into office by French cardinals. This was purely a European dispute and had nothing to do with the Holy Land. The leader of this so-called Crusade was the English Bishop of Norwich, Henry le Despenser. His army crossed the channel and besieged Ypres in 1383. A chronicler wrote that "having the banner of the Holy Cross before them...those who suffered death would be martyrs...and thus the blessing of the cross was achieved." Despenser's Crusade achieved nothing but death and destruction of fellow Christians. He abandoned the expedition and was subsequently impeached for his behavior.

This was not the end of the Church calling for Crusades against dissidents. On March 17, 1420, Pope Martin V issued a bull imploring the faithful to join in destroying dissident Christians or heretics belonging to the Wycliffite and Hussite sects in Bohemia. The Hussites were followers of the theologian Jan Hus, who was influenced by the writings of John Wycliffe and who was excommunicated by the Catholic Church and then burnt at the stake in 1415 for his heretical views on the presence of the body of Christ in Holy Communion. The King of Hungary, Germany, and Bohemia, Sigismund of Luxembourg, responding to Pope Martin's call for Crusade and assembled a large army of European knights and laid siege to the city of Prague, then the center of the Hussite rebellion against canonical Catholicism. Sigismund's Crusade was halted with a series of battlefield victories by the Hussites beginning in 1420. Four more calls by the papacy for Crusades against the Hussites failed to result in a victory of the Catholic Church over the Bohemian heretics. While some of those who took the cross in the struggle against the Hussites may have been genuinely motivated by a desire to protect the canonical doctrines of the Church, most of the knights and indeed Sigismund himself were driven by purely secular intentions—Sigismund to expand his power and the knights to increase their wealth through looting.

The decline of enthusiasm for Crusades by European leaders was a result of the evolution of medieval society following the fall of Acre in 1291 that occurred after the Ninth Crusade. Crusading was an expensive undertaking, and funds for adventuring in the Near East became more and more difficult to obtain. Such finances that could be raised for war were more effectively spent pursuing territorial expansion in Europe itself.

With the rise in power of independent city-states in Italy and proto-democratic urban centers in northern Europe, there was a gradual transference of power from aristocratic noble families, whose wealth was derived from agriculture, to urban merchant families. The notion of knightly honor slowly became fossilized so that it was acted out in tournaments, which were far less dangerous than fighting in a far-off land against unpredictable enemies using unpredictable tactics and more and more effective weapons. Wars did occur in Europe, and there were many, which typically tended to be internecine struggles or civil wars. The authority of the papacy also gradually declined as the Church became embroiled in struggles against heretical sects and eventually various forms of Protestantism.

In sum, the Crusades offered a religiously justified adventure for European knights and common folk. When successful, the lands acquired in the Near East by the Crusader knights were insufficient to support a stable noble lifestyle. Not only were the incomes derived from the estates in the East negligible as compared to what could be expected on European soil, but their defense was also extraordinarily costly in terms of lives and money. Without a long-term guarantee of subsidies from Europe, the Crusader knights were incapable of holding their estates and defending the Kingdom of Jerusalem. The arrival of the Mongols in Europe resulted in the expansion of their empire, which lasted from 1236 to 1242, and included most of Eastern Europe, then much of the Balkans, and later Anatolia; this just meant that there was yet another danger to be faced in the East. The idea of Crusading in the Holy Land became more and more impractical in terms of victory on the battlefield by European soldiers. If anything, the Crusades proved that there was no place for Europeans in the Levant.

Here are some other Captivating History books you might be interested in

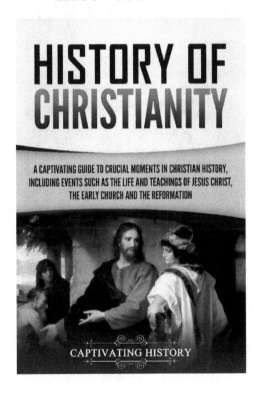

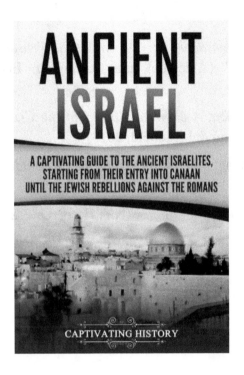

ANCIENT ISRAEL

A CAPTIVATING GUIDE TO THE ANCIENT ISRAELITES,
STARTING FROM THEIR ENTRY INTO CANAAN
UNTIL THE JEWISH REBELLIONS AGAINST THE ROMANS

CAPTIVATING HISTORY

Further Reading

Jaroslav Folda, *Crusader Art: The Art of the Crusaders in the Holy Land, 1099-1291* (Aldershot and Burlington: Lund Humphries, 2008)

Thomas F. Madden, *A Concise History of the Crusades*. (Lanham: Maryland: Rowman & Littlefield, 2013)

Steven Runciman, *A History of the Crusades*. (Cambridge: University Press, 1954)

Rodney Stark, *God's Battalions*, (NY: HarperOne, 2009)

Christopher Tyerman, *God's War: A New History of the Crusades*. (Harvard University Press, 2006